MUCKRAKING: PAST, PRESENT, AND FUTURE

MUCKRAKING

PAST

PRESENT

AND

FUTURE

Edited by JOHN M. HARRISON
and HARRY H. STEIN
Foreword by Irving Dilliard

THE PENNSYLVANIA STATE UNIVERSITY PRESS

UNIVERSITY PARK AND LONDON

Library of Congress Cataloging in Publication Data
Main entry under title:

Muckraking: past, present, and future.

Includes papers presented at a conference held at
Pennsylvania State University, May 14–16, 1970.
1. United States—Politics and government—20th
century—Addresses, essays, lectures. 2. United
States—Social conditions—Addresses, essays, lectures.
3. Journalism—United States—Addresses, essays,
lectures. I. Harrison, John M., ed. II. Stein,
Harry H., 1938– ed.
E743.M82   320.9'73'09   73–11204
ISBN 0–271–01118–1

CONTENTS

PREFACE

This volume was inspired by the response to the conference on "Muckraking: Past, Present, and Future," held at The Pennsylvania State University, May 14–16, 1970, with the editors serving as cochairmen.

The idea of such a conference emerged from a continuing series of discussions, growing out of our mutual concerns with muckraking and muckrakers as a historical phenomenon. We were aware, too, of mounting evidence that a kind of journalism much like that which had flourished early in this century was enjoying a vigorous revival. The term "muckraking" was being used with increasing frequency about many reporters and authors. The time seemed ripe for exploration of both the historical and the contemporary manifestations of muckraking.

Substantial contributions to the financial support of the conference, from which many of the materials for this book were drawn, were made by its cosponsors—the School of Journalism, the Department of History, and the American Studies Program. Additional funds were provided by other units of The Pennsylvania State University: the Institute for the Arts and Humanistic Studies, the Center for Continuing Liberal Education, the Liberal Arts Research Office, and the Department of English. A grant from the Stern Fund (New York City) helped greatly in meeting various expenses, including a subvention for publication of this book.

A revised version of the paper by Carey McWilliams, which appears here, and portions of the paper by Dr. Nathan B. Blumberg appeared in the *Columbia Journalism Review* (Autumn, 1970).

We are indebted to many others who lent support and encouragement to the conference and to publication of this book.

JOHN M. HARRISON
HARRY H. STEIN

Six Decades Later

Irving Dilliard

Justice Oliver Wendell Holmes was elevated to the Supreme Court in 1902. That same year Editor S. S. McClure chanced to put together the historic issue of his monthly magazine presenting articles by Ida M. Tarbell, Ray Stannard Baker, and Lincoln Steffens on separate but not altogether unrelated wrongs in the United States of America at the opening of the twentieth century.

Justice Holmes was nominated to the highest tribunal by Theodore Roosevelt. This was the very same president who would chastise the Tarbells, Bakers, and Steffenses—along with such coworkers as David Graham Phillips and Upton Sinclair, Charles E. Russell and Samuel Hopkins Adams—as beneficial to the well-being of society "but only if they know when to stop raking the muck." The protesting president was reaching back to the Man with the Muck-rake in *The Pilgrim's Progress*, who, so John Bunyan wrote, was unable to see "the celestial crown" held out for him, who "could look no way but downwards" . . . who "raked to himself the straws, the small sticks and the dust of the floor."

More than a decade and a half before that January, 1903 issue of *McClure's* magazine, Judge Holmes of Massachusetts had described the motivation as well as the fate of the crusading journalists who were to dig deeply into the questionable practices of those burgeoning times. To be somewhat more specific, into such diverse areas as industrial corporations, insurance companies, and railroads; into financial controls, patent medicines, and harmful drugs; into municipal corruption, commercialized vice, and racial discrimination; into unemployment and poverty, into the judicial system and indeed into the press itself. Appearing as an esteemed alumnus of the Harvard Class of 1861, already a veteran of life as he was also a veteran of Ball's Bluff, Antietam and Fredericksburg, Holmes spoke these words to an assembly of undergraduates at Harvard College on February 17, 1886:

. . . No man has earned the right to intellectual ambition until he has learned to lay his course by a star which he has never seen—to dig by a divining rod for springs he may never reach. In saying this, I point to that which will make your study heroic. For I say to you in all sadness of conviction, that to think great thoughts you must be heroes as well as idealists. Only when you have worked alone—when you have felt around you the black gulf of solitude more isolating than that which surrounds the dying man, and in hope and in despair have trusted to your own unshaken will—then only will you have achieved. Thus only can you gain the secret isolated joy of the thinker, who knows that a hundred years after he is dead and forgotten, men who never heard of him will be moving to the measure of his thought—the subtle rapture of a postponed power, which the world knows not because it has no external trappings, but which to his prophetic vision is more real than that which commands an army. And if this joy should not be yours, still it is only thus that you can know that you have done what it lay in you to do—can say that you have lived, and be ready for the end.

The "secret isolated joy of the thinker" who knows that long after he is gone men will be "moving to the measure of his thought"—that was the way it would be with that company of practical idealists whom the Man in the White House in effect misnamed the "Muckrakers" in 1906. To be sure they did rake the muck at their feet but only as the necessary first step in clearing that muck away. As they labored, they lifted their eyes to the heavens of a cleaner world.

Now, sixty years afterward, it is rather fashionable to say that the muck-rakers failed, that although they did light up the sky of the first decade of our century, it was only for a short time and little was left to show for their labors. Let those who will so read the record, but let them make certain they have the full report at hand. For there are others who find a body of accomplishment that, in the telling verb of Justice Holmes, we *move* to today.

This book is, in this observer's eyes, clearly on the side of achievement of a most significant kind. Indeed if the handiwork of the muckraking journalists had come to naught there now would be no such volume as this one.

Most journalists are unwilling to dismiss the muckraking movement as a failure, though there still are many who seek to date it quite firmly from 1902 to 1912 and then draw the drapes of history securely thereafter. That 1902 is too late can be established quickly enough. For it was exactly a full decade earlier that Edward W. Bok caused the *Ladies' Home Journal* to announce that it would print no more patent medicine advertisements. And in 1892, as for years afterward, the nostrum-makers with their siren songs were a chief source of magazine revenue.

Bok, who had emigrated from the Netherlands at the age of seven, took up his publishing duties on Cyrus H. K. Curtis' new and venturesome monthly in Philadelphia in October, 1889. These began, not without significance, almost coincidentally with the opening of Hull House in Chicago by Jane Addams. Through the dozen closing years of the century, Bok forced the light of his pages into one dark place after another. Problems that urgently needed illumination got it in his "female magazine," as not a few male editors tagged it in ridicule.

But Bok knew the needs of the times better than his detractors. Thus he had no competition when he took up, in the *Ladies' Home Journal*, the long forbidden topic of venereal disease. That brought on a fearful storm and not a few offended readers canceled their subscriptions. The pressure also led to the withdrawal of no little advertising. All this reaction Bok accepted as to be expected by the editorial pioneer. Thus he became the first editor to discard the long-standing taboo against mention of venereal disease in a journal with national distribution.

At the same time Bok and his writers could see what was happening in the cities and on the land. So they campaigned for municipal renovation, for the conservation of natural resources, and for a healthy environment— in short, for the ecology, to use a word that would become part of the common speech three-quarters of a century later.

Yet pioneer with the printed page that Edward Bok was, he had his predecessors. Consider Jacob A. Riis. An even earlier emigrant from Denmark, Riis tried his hand and perfected his English on a weekly newspaper at Hunter's Point, Long Island. Then he got on at the *New York Tribune* in 1877 as police headquarters reporter. Until 1888 on the daily that Greeley had done so much to shape and then on Dana's *New York Sun* until 1899, this newcomer to our shores put most native-born citizens to shame with his intense concern for the well-being of their precious heritage.

For Jacob Riis was not content to report the police blotter news of accidents and crime and violence that took him into the slums. He literally declared his own personal war on the tenement districts. His fight certainly was not against the wretched people in the rude rooms with cracking walls. It was leveled at the exploiting employers and landlords who were so largely responsible for the physical, moral, and spiritual degredation of thousands of the city's men, women, and children.

Riis had both the determination and the constitution for revealing the sorry contents, human and material, of these ghettoes. By showing what their surroundings were doing to the young, Riis stirred hundreds of sympathetic readers who joined his attack with energy, with influence—and with funds.

The slums did not disappear overnight, but some of the worst came down to provide space for school playgrounds. He demanded and he got lights for dark tenement hallways. His proof of the contamination of the Manhattan water supply was the starting point for the acquisition of the Croton watershed. If he alone could have abolished child labor he would have done so gladly. But since he could not, he did what he could: he launched an almost unbroken succession of campaigns for the prohibitory legislation that would be enacted years later in Washington and Albany and other capitals.

Let it be underscored that Jacob A. Riis' years as a police reporter on the *New York Tribune* and the *New York Sun*, when he also was leading these heroic one-man crusades, embraced nearly a quarter-century, from 1877 to 1899. His earliest books, *How the Other Half Lives* and *The Children of the Poor*, appeared respectively in 1890 and 1892, and their very titles make evident how pioneering they were.

As for the years since 1912, Messrs. Harrison and Stein, who had the perspective to assemble this collection of essays, cite many latter day muckrakers in their contributions to this book. One mentioned in the first chapter made a strong impression on the present writer in the 1920s. He was Paul Y. Anderson.

Born outside Knoxville, Tennessee in 1893, Anderson worked nearly the whole of his restless newspaperman's life on the *St. Louis Post-Dispatch*. But he had one period of freelance reporting in Washington, from 1923 to 1924 during the Harding Era, and it was then that Anderson began to pursue with scrupulous care the Senate investigation of the transfers of the Teapot Dome and Elk Hills naval oil reserves. His dispatches were outstanding for their penetration into the very heart of the scandalous favoritism that underlay the transfers. How helpful Anderson's relentless digging was to truth in government in a democracy became clear beyond any doubt when the chairman of the Senate committee conducting the inquiry, Senator Thomas J. Walsh of Montana, generously acknowledged the debt of the public to the freelance reporter. Anderson followed every trail that he came onto, with the result that faithless men in high places were brought low in a striking demonstration of what a free, probing newsman can help achieve.

This independent work by Paul Y. Anderson so impressed the *Post-Dispatch*'s managing editor, Oliver K. Bovard, that he rehired his former staff member, established him in the paper's Washington Bureau, and encouraged him to expose official skullduggery countless times after that. At Anderson's death, he was described as "probably the last of the Muckrakers" by Oswald Garrison Villard, editor of *The Nation*, formerly with the New York *Evening Post*, and himself a persevering cleanser of the national scene. Whether his description was wholly accurate, Villard sought to pay Anderson a high tribute as a newspaper crusader with a long list of accomplishments of benefit to the people.

The spirit of Anderson was the spirit of the *Post-Dispatch* when this writer joined its staff as bottom-rung reporter late in that same decade of the '20s. City Editor Ben H. Reese, sending the brand new cub to cover Police Court as an early assignment, told the beginner substantially this:

"Something is wrong over at Police Court. Something is always wrong over there. What is wrong now, we don't know. It is up to the *Post-Dispatch* reporter to find out what it is and get it into the paper."

The city editor's instruction, in just about those words, comes back so vividly that it might have been said last week instead of nearly fifty years ago. Yet it must be noted that although the investigative spirit may have had an unusual intensity at the *Post-Dispatch*, it was not unique at Twelfth and Olive in St. Louis. The *Post-Dispatch*, its publisher and its editors, its correspondents and reporters did not possess that spirit exclusively. There were other newspaper editors, for example, William Allen White of the Emporia (Kansas) *Gazette* and William T. Evjue of the Madison (Wisconsin) *Capital Times*, and magazine editors such as Villard, who set out on courses from which they would not turn back. To be sure, there were not nearly as many as there should have been, but enough to keep muckraking alive in the land and to show what it could do when it was practiced with intelligence and determination. Again, the names of not a few of these are called up by the editors of this book in their summary chapter.

But, after all, just what did the muckrakers really accomplish?

One way or another, are not many, if not most, of the problems that they took up still with us?

Did they do more than call attention to conditions that needed correction?

What problems did they solve?

What of permanence remains?

These questions can only mean that the time has come to make absolutely certain that all doubters have access to the career of David Graham Phillips, at least in capsule form. For in his short span of fewer than forty-five years, Phillips influenced American politics, American finance and American society in ways given to not too many other of his or any time. Here is his record in brief:

David Graham Phillips was born in the Ohio River port town of Madison, Indiana in 1867. By the age of twelve he had read all the Dickens, Scott, and Hugo that he could get his hands on. He had been through the Bible several times. Shakespeare was not far off. His father had gone to Methodist Asbury College—later DePauw—in Greencastle, Indiana, and so sent his promising son there. Phillips promptly met an older student named Albert J. Beveridge, who would become a leading Progressive in the United States Senate. Their friendship was immediate and lasting. At Asbury the two passed many evenings together, trying out their ideas and views on each other and discussing the issues of the hour.

With Beveridge's graduation in 1885, Phillips transferred, largely for the experience of living in the East, to the College of New Jersey in Princeton—not yet bearing its later name—for his third and fourth years. He spoke up forcefully in contests in Whig Hall, achieved a high scholastic record, and was graduated in 1887. Barely a month later he became a reporter on the Cincinnati *Times-Star*. After being bid away by the competing *Commercial Gazette*, he remained in Cincinnati three years and then went in 1890 to Dana's *New York Sun*.

Phillips' enterprise as a news gatherer came to the attention of Joseph Pulitzer, who, as editor and publisher of the New York *World*, always had his eye out for fresh talent. Pulitzer arranged to hire young Phillips away from Dana and before long had him at work on a news investigation that stirred up the New York financial world and then reached out over the country. Gigantic business combinations were not being prosecuted under the Sherman Anti-Trust Act. Phillips produced a major series of articles flaying the trusts and calling their operations to the attention of the United States attorney general. Each Phillips exposé would close with the statement: "Such, Mr. Olney, are the facts, and here, sir, is the law." Then came a pertinent provision of the federal law.

Although Pulitzer had Phillips in mind for a post of high responsibility on the *World*, the young reporter developed other plans for his life and work. He wanted to reach a broader audience than was possible through one newspaper, so he began writing for the popular magazines, then coming into unprecedented prominence. In the first years of the new century he published in *Everybody's* monthly articles with one provocative title after another: "Swollen Fortunes," "The Man Who Made the Money

Trust," "The Madness of Much Power," "The Power Behind the Throne."
Then, in March 1906, exploded the first of Phillips' sensational series,
"The Treason of the Senate," in William Randolph Hearst's *Cosmopolitan*.

The nine installments opened with an expose of the numerous corporate
connections of Senator Chauncey M. Depew of New York. That the story-
telling Senator was up to his mutton-chop whiskers in business enterprise
could not be gainsaid. He was on at least seventy boards of directors, and
there could be little question as to why he had been put on them. Still the
disclosures and the way they were phrased were painful to his old friend
in the White House, Theodore Roosevelt. The president, after having
earlier expressed his defensive sentiments at an unreported dinner of the
Washington correspondents' Gridiron Club, used the cornerstone laying
for the House of Representatives building, April 14, 1906, as the occasion
to speak publicly of the crusading writers as, in effect, men with Bunyan's
muckrake.

Senator Depew and his New York colleague, Thomas C. Platt, were
described by Phillips as having been chosen by the state legislature at Albany "by and for the interests" to join "the senatorial rank and file of dili-
gent, faithful enemies of their country." Nelson W. Aldrich of Rhode
Island, Henry Cabot Lodge of Massachusetts, William B. Allison of Iowa,
Joseph B. Foraker of Ohio, Arthur P. Gorman of Maryland and many
other Senators of the day came off little better at Phillips' hands. For years,
one Wisconsin senator had been said to represent the lumber interests of
the state, the other its railroads, while the ordinary people came out at a
very short end. Thus what David Graham Phillips wrote about the "most
powerful club on earth" was closer than it should have been to the sorry
truth.

Chauncey Depew's friend in the White House was not the only one
who found fault with the Phillips series. There were others who read the
articles as intemperate. Some believed that, though solid criticism was in
order, it was going too far to charge senators with treason within the
meaning of the Constitution. Although his impact was far greater than he
realized, Phillips was both disappointed and disturbed by this adverse
reaction. Now he turned from the revelations of the day in the popular
magazines to the writing of novels on still another major concern—the
submerged place of women in American life.

In a succession of works of fiction, Phillips focused the attention of a
steadily increasing readership on the second-class position occupied by
women and undertook to make the case for a new equality. In one situa-

tion or another this was the common problem of *The Social Secretary*, *The Hungry Heart*, *The Husband's Story*, and *The Price She Paid*, all published between 1905 and 1912. But Phillips set his greatest store by *Susan Lenox: Her Fall and Rise*, which he completed near the end of his life, but which was not released until 1917—some six years after his death. Although little mentioned now, *Susan Lenox* was the bitter yet triumphant story of a beautiful woman in a corrupt and exploiting society. For months it was a major topic of discussion. Feminists, clergymen, editors, critics, educators—all joined in the national debate set off by the publication of Phillips' posthumous novel.

What David Graham Phillips had done was to lay a significant part of the groundwork for the submission and ratification of three historic amendments to the United States Constitution. In the order of their adoption, these were:

The Sixteenth Amendment, submitted by Congress in 1909 and ratified by the states in 1913. This amendment wrote into the Constitution congressional authority for the levy and collection of federal income taxes. Thanks to this amendment, the controllers of the money power were required to provide, for the first time, a more equitable share of the revenue needed by an industrialized society. Phillips notably helped to create the necessary public opinion in support of the amendment through his newspaper and magazine articles that laid open the financial manipulations previously so largely hidden from the eyes of ordinary men and women.

The Seventeenth Amendment, submitted in 1912 and ratified in 1913. This amendment changed the method by which United States senators were chosen. Beginning with the adoption of the Constitution in 1788, senators had been elected by the legislatures of the states they represented. Too often these elections had been marked by scandal, sometimes by outright purchase. This amendment took senatorial elections out of boss-ridden legislatures and made them the responsibility of the voters in the states. Phillips' articles on "The Treason of the Senate," anticipating as they did the shocking Lorimer Case in Illinois, were an incentive to overdue correction.

The Nineteenth Amendment, submitted in 1919 and ratified in 1920. This amendment prohibited discrimination on the basis of sex in voting for president, for vice president, and for senators and representatives in Congress. There can be no question that Phillips' persistent writing for a large popular audience on the subject of the political, economic and social mistreatment of women in the United States helped to bring about this major constitutional change.

David Graham Phillips did not live to see the full contribution of his efforts. Shots fired by a deranged man cut him down outside New York's Princeton Club on January 23, 1911. He died the next day, not yet forty-four years old. If the students of our politics knew more of the history of our journalism and the historians of our journalism paid more attention to political change and development, this tragically short career would be far better known and more fully appreciated. Indeed Phillips long ago would have become associated with the adoption of these *three* major amendments to the Constitution, instead of essentially at this writing for the first time.

Yet Phillips was only one in that wide-ranging company of journalistic pioneers. Remember that Jacob A. Riis campaigned more than three-quarters of a century ago for lighted hallways in the tenements as a means of combating crime in New York City. Then note the following front-page headline that appeared in the *Wall Street Journal* of April 18, 1973:

LIGHT IN THE HALLWAY

CRIME AND FEAR DECLINE
AS TENANTS TAKE OVER
HOUSING DEVELOPMENT

Under this heading, correspondent Liz Roman Gallese offered a staff report on how Boston's Bromley-Heath public housing development was being reclaimed by its Tenant Management Corporation, after life at the residential complex had descended to "the bottom of the barrel." For Linda Taylor, twenty-three, mother of two, and afraid to leave her apartment for fear of burglary, TMC "put a light in a hall stairway." Because this had to be done seven to eight decades after Riis obtained his hallway light regulation, should the gloomy judgment be passed that the muckrakers were a flash in the pan, that they failed, that little or nothing of their handiwork remained for anyone to see? On the contrary, let them be saluted for foresight, for perception, for vision, for leadership. And if not every hall or stairway built thereafter contained the light it needed, what about those three constitutional amendments that came out of a public opinion formed in substantial part by the crusades of David Graham Phillips?

As this is written, the secrecy and coverup around the criminal acts of break-in and theft at the Democratic National Headquarters in the 1972 presidential campaign are falling apart like a house built with bits of cardboard. Give the credit not to the "open," self-proclaimed "law and order" Nixon administration, but to the press. The *Washington Post* in particular, but also other newspapers, including notably the *New York Times*, the *Los Angeles Times*, the *Christian Science Monitor* and, in certain respects, the *Wall Street Journal*, and their publishers, editors, and reporters deserve the nation's gratitude. This holds for the weekly news magazines, *Time* and *Newsweek*, and their staffs. Again it was the *Washington Post* that was not dissuaded but continued to dig for the facts, even in the face of the White House's barrage of ridicule and pious professions that the long silent president had nothing to hide. The presidential press secretary became not a cooperating facilitator of the needs of the press in its quest for the truth for the American people, but a misleader of the media, their readers and listeners.

These new exposures and revelations by the press are the best of omens. They can go far to overcome damage done to our democracy by faithless officials, both elected and appointed. Let this muckraking go on and on and on. Then democracy will shake off its betrayers and a new era of beneficial protections will come with brighter days for public service and political health.

How could there be a more appropriate recognition of the accomplishments of muckrakers Phillips, Tarbell, and Sinclair; Russell, Adams, Baker, and Steffens; and all their fellow laborers?

How could there be?

Muckraking Journalism in Twentieth-Century America

Harry H. Stein and John M. Harrison

What is muckraking? The question has been asked many times since the day in 1906 when President Theodore Roosevelt distorted John Bunyan's description of the man with the muckrake and applied it to a group of writers—most of them journalists—in popular magazines and newspapers. Attempts to answer the question have been many and varied, but none has gained general acceptance and approval to this day. "Muckraking" was an ugly term, often a smear word, and it came to summon up still uglier associations in the minds of many individuals when applied to the American press.

Muckraking has evoked strong, even visceral reactions because it has dealt with the kinds of issues in this century—prison conditions, abuse of political office, and economic exploitation, for instance—that nearly guarantee such evocations. The muckrakers' words and images have aimed at the penetration of popular ignorance and fatalism to make suffering vivid and indignities real to uninvolved citizens. So muckrakers inevitably have had to defend against libel actions, economic pressures, individual and community harassment, and corrosive private doubts as to their own effectiveness.

President Lyndon Johnson on October 21, 1964, equated muckraking with "slanderous comment or mudslinging" and assured voters that the American people "will not listen to 'muckraking'." Muckraking was identified with "throwing mud and garbage" and "getting into the gutter" in Senator Barry Goldwater's successful libel suit against magazine publisher Ralph Ginzburg. One newspaper editor in the 1950s typically ordered reporters to boost their town, help the paper make money, and "confine muckraking to bitching about taxes." According to one account, the "muckraker" is a recognizable social type in the popular language: he is the troublemaker.[1]

Thus detractors have variously associated muckraking with yellow journalism, narrow partisanship, and sensationalism, or with pandering to base human instincts and causes. It has been characterized as a splenetic distortion of reality, intended to convey falsehoods, remaining silent about—or discounting—positive good in American society. Such characterizations have militated against exact definition and assessment of muckraking as well as its practice.

In sharp contrast, muckraking has received extensive praise. A leader of the sit-in which rocked Columbia University in 1968 asserted that "the muckraking function of the press" provides the "last avenue of protest before more drastic action." Without the press protesting social evils, "the country is in for a hard time and we're all in very deep difficulty," he warned. Even former White House adviser Daniel P. Moynihan, in the context of blaming muckrakers today for weakening the legitimate authority of the presidency, grudgingly allows, "Few would want to be without the [muckraking] tradition, and it is the young journalist of poor spirit who does not set out to uncover the machinations of some malefactor of great wealth and his political collaborators." Journalists have consistently been the strongest proponents of muckraking. Large and important publications and aspirants to such stature have variously announced themselves muckraking organs in this century. Pulitzer Prizes and like awards have repeatedly gone to muckrakers. And the possibilities of democratic persuasion inherent in muckraking have always attracted novelists, artists, lawyers, social workers, and public officials—men like Brand Whitlock, Benjamin B. Lindsey, and Ralph Nader—who have broadened the perspectives afforded by professional journalists. Obviously, there are powerful traditions in the mass media and in American life which sustain the prestige of a journalism of conscience which some have labeled muckraking and others, less properly, have named crusading or public-interest journalism.[2]

Some have argued that the definition of muckraking depends on the political and ideological sympathies of those who do the defining. Was the now-defunct *Scanlan's Monthly* correct in alleging in July, 1970, that *Life,* cited as a muckraking organ in its waning years, actually masqueraded in that role while serving as a conduit for information obtained illegally by the United States Department of Justice? What weight must be given such publications as *Human Events* and *The News in Review*, with its John Birch Society connections, which purport to expose Communist conspiracies to fluoridate water supplies or to brainwash school children? Do the means or the ends determine what is and what is not muckraking journalism?

Several factors, apart from the emotive term itself, contribute to the difficulty of arriving at a single definition of muckraking, one that will be acceptable to its actual and potential contributors, to its audience, and to its students. There is, for example, the variety of shapes it has taken in the various media. The primary focus in this book is on muckraking in the journalistic media—magazines, newspapers, and, more recently, radio and television. But as muckraking messages have been sent through many communications channels, some recognition must also be paid to muckraking in literature, in volumes of social analysis, in newsletters, and in such forms as cartoons and photographs. The muckraking novel, poem, play, movie, and formal social critique are important in their own right and for their often close association with muckraking journalism. They should be the subject of future scrutiny if the full impact of the muckraking phenomenon is ever to be understood.

Muckraking has been a phenomenon specific to the journalism of the United States. Its opportunities for practice and degree of popularity have always been related to conditions within the press and within the country. Muckraking has been a journalistic form continuously formed and re-formed by its creators, by its channels of communication, and by those who receive its messages. From decade to decade in the twentieth century none of these elements has remained exactly the same. The first spirited generation of muckrakers fell away prior to World War I and, with few exceptions, were not replaced in number or influence until the late 1960s and 1970s. Today, a new generation of practitioners has different views of the issues and different means of analyzing and expressing them from those of Lincoln Steffens, Ida Tarbell, Ray Stannard Baker, and other muckrakers of the Progressive Era. Yet they often share the assumptions of their illustrious predecessors just as they sometimes dwell on similar problems. The country has changed and so too the media available for muckraking and the publics actually or potentially receptive to it. Nevertheless, continuity exists between the journalism of conscience of the Progressive Era and that of the present.

Muckraking is associated with four major press traditions in America. It bears closest resemblance to investigative journalism; less, to advocacy journalism. It has a distant relation to sensationalistic and to yellow journalism. (A crucial mistake of proponents and detractors alike has been to equate muckraking with one or another of these American press traditions.) The work of investigation, like muckraking, furnishes a careful, accurate, inevitably non-neutral account and analysis in words and images of a set of events, ideas, circumstances, or persons. Both usually expose or reveal fresh facts or patterns of meaning to their audiences and sometimes offer solutions to depicted problems. Investigative journalism encompasses the "watchdog" function of the American press: the surveillance of governmental and political institutions and personnel and their conformance to ordinances and regulations and to social values and norms resembling law. Muckrakers exercise a surveillance over a wider area than government and politics and so have probed the unique and the common in American society, the highest reaches of power and the everyday social patterns of the population. Also, muckrakers sometimes define as a removable evil a practice or view normally accepted as natural, inescapable, or beneficent. By helping to enlarge Americans' expectations of what is possible and desirable in their lifetimes, they illuminate fundamental intentions both to inform and to improve their fellows. Furthermore, the muckraking work, already selective in facts and emphasis to elicit indignation or anger, proceeds beyond the investigative form to indicate how extensive, not unique, are the practices and ideas exposed. It denounces or praises specific individuals, conditions, or values, and exhorts its audience, explicitly or by tone, to "take action" or to support specific remedies. In a sense, muckrakers have insisted directly and investigative journalists indirectly that Americans concern themselves with the norms of public and individual good, the nature of existing realities and social change, and the standards and needs of a representative democracy. In that manner, both forms have become segments of extended social action, more so as their representatives have often engaged in public speaking and testifying, pamphleteering, unofficial advising of leaders, and other nonjournalistic activities.

To become a propagandist or apologist for a particular viewpoint or organization has always been a seductive danger for journalists of conscience. Still, they have never *fully* entered the stream of the oldest press tradition in America, that of advocacy journalism. This tradition has been represented by the factional and party newspapers of colonial and nineteenth-century America, by the pamphlets and other writings of Thomas Paine, Theodore Parker, William Lloyd Garrison, and Henry George, and by such twentieth-century magazines as the *Commoner, Masses, Progressive, Nation,* and *New Republic.* Little or no pretense to detachment or neutrality exists in advocacy journalism. Advocacy has been characterized by deliberate silence on some topics, suppression of material uncomplimentary to its partisans, and intentional bias in selection of subjects, emphasis, and interpretations. Muckrakers have resembled advocacy journalists in making emotional appeals, in personalizing complex issues, and in thus placing a premium on public opinion to right wrongs, defeat conspiracies, or alter institutions, attitudes, or values. The line between the two forms can blur, as in the collection of *Ramparts* articles, *Divided We Stand,* which its editors described in 1971 as "positive muckraking." Indeed, partisan outlets have been normal refuges for muckrakers lacking access to general-circulation media.

Distinct from advocacy journalists, muckrakers have tried to preserve their autonomy, never irretrievably commiting themselves to any single cause or person. They have checked their partisanship (but not their critical sensibilities) with a healthy skepticism, journalistic norms or instructions, and audience predilections. Supporting Theodore Roosevelt, they could, like Lincoln Steffens, praise Socialism and Robert M. La Follette and later shift support to Woodrow Wilson. Drew Pearson and Jack Anderson have spurred federal officials regardless of party. In the television documentaries, "Hunger in America" and "This Child Is Rated X," muckraking newsmen have not simply operated as spokesmen for liberal senators on charges that hunger and child abuse are routine in the United States. They verified, extended, and deepened the senators' charges and broadcast them to a national audience. But if they become too evenhanded or detached, muckrakers, as those connected with the magazine *KEN* learned by 1940, will never build a following.[3]

Finally, sensationalistic journalism and its extension into a yellow journalism which manufactures news, banners misleading headlines, and luridly illustrates its stories have a few parallels with muckraking. Hearst, Pulitzer, and their many imitators treated subjects like scandal and corruption, sex, and violence in a provocative manner and in doing so touched the often inchoate needs and aspirations of millions of Americans. Sensationalism figured prominently in the muckraking of ex-New York *World* city editor Charles Edward Russell, less so in muckraking by his contemporaries before World War I. Like sensationalistic and yellow journalism, muckraking has supported political and social crusades, focused on nongenteel subjects, and adopted such techniques as human-interest stories to win attention and sympathy. The immense audience for the muckraking in the syndicated "Washington Merry-Go-Round" column since the 1930s might be due partly to the late Drew Pearson's and Jack Anderson's use of tantalizing gossip and slangy language. Nevertheless, while the sensationalistic and yellow journalist exposes in order to entertain and titillate Americans, the muckraker labors to offer them a profound and specific education. Muckrakers distinguish, examine, and judge whatever has seemed to improve or lessen humankind and society. The thrust for moral social improvement is part of their design.

Muckraking was very prominent in the American media from about 1902 to 1912 and became so again in the late 1960s. During the intervening years isolated voices called for a resurgent muckraking, presented agendas for investigation, and bemoaned the lack of observable journalistic response. Even throughout the tumult of the 1930s, journalism neither manifested a serious muckraking phenomenon nor accorded distinction to muckraking, despite the extensive social criticism—some of it muckraking—in the plastic and graphic arts, in fiction and nonfictional books, and in other forms. For instance, mass-circulation newspapers, radio stations, and magazines assiduously ignored the fight for a more stringent pure food and drug law. The *Ladies' Home Journal, Collier's,* and the newspapers which had helped arouse Americans to the need for the original federal regulation were silent in the 1930s. Those who muckraked the food and drug industry, according to one account, were forced to reach "their public through books and slender-circulation magazines." A pervasive mass mood of disaffection with the social order (and a corollary disposition toward beneficent change), which *Nation* editor Carey McWilliams argues in this book is needed to actuate and spread the influence of muckraking, simply did not translate into a Depression revival of muckraking journalism, except possibly for Pearson's newspaper column. Nor were times of relative affluence in these intervening years much better for the lonely muckraking of Upton Sinclair, Paul Y. Anderson of the St. Louis *Post-Dispatch,* Albert Deutsch of New York's *PM,* and others.[4]

Early in the century muckrakers had recognized that a sense of uneasiness about the malfunctioning political, economic, and social institutions which had begun to become evident several decades earlier was troubling increasing numbers of Americans. They found the medium for the message—more precisely, perhaps, the medium found them—in the popular magazines that represented one current manifestation of the communications revolution that had begun at least half a century earlier. An audience was there, and the means for reaching it was at hand. The muckrakers availed themselves of that fortuituous combination.

Similar circumstances existed by the late 1960s. By 1971 a national opinion poll by Potomac Associates revealed that two-thirds of the respondents were dissatisfied with the status quo, lacked confidence in political institutions and their leaders, and believed the United States had regressed in the last five years. Americans were again receptive in large numbers, and again muckrakers found extensive channels for addressing them. To reach the minds and hearts of the people in terms of the root problems of the current malaise became a great challenge.

They took it up with the same fervor and robust spirit as the muckrakers of the pre-World War I era. Some of the problems, like political corruption and economic exploitation, were almost identical with those discussed in the earlier time. Others, including American activities abroad, were fresh issues. New audiences were detected in youth, in those of non-middle-class life styles, even in the masses watching television and reading general-circulation periodicals. New magazines like *Ramparts* and *Scanlan's Monthly* offered channels of communication. The *Washington Monthly* developed with Ralph Nader a sponsorship of "the whistleblower, the muckraker from within, who exposes what he considers the unconscionable practices of his own organization."[5] And such periodicals as the *Saturday Evening Post* and *Life*, which normally spurned muckraking, now opened their pages to it. On December 15, 1967, at the signing of the Wholesome Meat Act, President Johnson would pay tribute to a group of journalists whose investigations and muckraking articles had inspired the new law and to an invited Upton Sinclair, whose *The Jungle* symbolized continuity with the past. Ignoring his 1964 attack on muckraking, the Chief Executive assured listeners that "the good people of America will always respond when they have the facts and when they hear a responsible call to action."

Pondering muckraking works since the late 1960s and the evaluations offered by muckrakers in this book, one can recognize that present-day muckrakers, as much as their predecessors, are committed to changes that will effect progress. They hold, sometimes ambivalently, to a faith in the ultimate rationality of men and women to make needed changes once confronted with full documentation of human and institutional error and defect. Yet today's muckrakers seem more cognizant of the intricacies of social change, more skeptical about the universality of their judgments and values, less expectant of quick and inevitably beneficent results than such earlier muckrakers as Thomas W. Lawson, Mark Sullivan, and George Creel. Steffens, Tarbell, and Sinclair, the editors of the *Washington Monthly* believe, had only scattered corruption to face, while Ralph Nader and his contemporaries face such all-pervasive corruption that their muckraking has to it "a somber cast" and represents only "a promise of possible reform, a tentative hope. . . ."[6] Indeed, muckrakers now are less likely than their predecessors to perceive evidence of public and media interest in their messages as a great new popular awakening. The mass public moved to great acts by a journalism of conscience, they think a rarity or impossibility. Some consequently appeal only to narrow segments of opinion or to "opinion-makers." However, their quickness to blame cowardly, uncaring, or venal publishers, editors, and advertisers for constraints on their revelations has not changed.

Much has been said in this book and elsewhere regarding the public which muckraking has enjoyed or could potentially enjoy. In 1914 Walter Lippmann wrote in *Drift and Mastery* that "the mere fact that muckraking was what the people wanted to hear is in many ways the most important revelation of the whole campaign" the nation had just witnessed. Lippmann suggested that muckrakers had won quick approval because they both illuminated the real causes of public dissatisfaction and gave the appearance of doing something about them.[7] Since the 1900s the muckrakers themselves have held a motivating premise that somewhere in the United States there existed a concerned, disquieted audience receptive to their messages. Any responsiveness by their *own* constituencies also has concerned individuals frequently touched by the work of muckrakers—the public officials, the corporation executives, the managers of competing communication media. They must ask if the number or influence of those actually or potentially roused by muckraking can safely be ignored or whether it is better to mount a prosecution, pass a law, launch an inquiry, initiate a publicity campaign, or change editorial direction. Like the muckraker, they too must be keenly interested in what public is being cultivated by muckraking.

Significant disagreements about the nature of the muckrakers' audience have occurred repeatedly and lead to differing conceptions of muckraking. The disagreements echo in this book. To Louis Filler, for example, muckraking in this century is an appeal to the conscience of the American middle class, which may be approximated with today's "silent majority." It is a message directed toward achievement of a kind of consensus concerning the needs and goals of a society. To Nathan Blumberg and James Higgins, on the other hand, muckraking is an assault upon the accepted values of that same "middle America." If it is not avowedly revolutionary, certainly it does not shrink from the possibility of revolution should other means of effecting change fail. Filler's muckraking is, in most respects, poles apart from that of Blumberg and Higgins. They are different messages, communicated to different audiences, intended to achieve different ends.

Most commentators and practitioners believe that the urban middle class has furnished the fundamental audience for muckraking in any decade of this century. A small following from the middle class persists whatever the national mood and whatever the inclinations of the bulk of middle-class Americans. The permanent following includes people who sympathized with Sinclair's muckraking in the 1920s and with I.F. Stone's in the 1950s, supporters of two small contemporary newspapers, the *Texas Observer* and the San Francisco *Bay Guardian*, and adherents to the muckraking appearing for many years in the small-circulation *New Republic* and *Nation*. Twice—from about 1902 to 1912 and again since the late 1960s (though support may now be dwindling)—muckraking has had an upsurge, thanks partly to the enthusiasm of a larger and more influential following from within the middle class. Finally, it is believed, a mass audience cutting across residence and class has been realized occasionally by muckrakers in this century when their efforts appeared in large-circulation newspapers or magazines or on television.

This overall conception may hide some important audiences of muckraking. Trade unionists belonging to the C.I.O. supported the muckraking newsletter *In Fact* in the 1940s. Working people admired Judge Ben Lindsey's muckraking of juvenile delinquency and crime before World War I. The Chicago *Daily News* and St. Louis *Post-Dispatch*, which printed muckraking for years, circulate in large metropolitan regions, reaching small and large communities, including the homes of readers who are distinctly not middle-class. The national interest tapped by exposures in the now-defunct *Saturday Evening Post* and *Life* magazines of criminal-political connections, by *Ramparts'* muckraking, and by particular television documentaries suggest a reservoir of responsiveness to muckraking not coterminous with the urban middle class. It is likely that muckraking addressed to *every* American has always been doomed not to be heard by these millions. It seems equally probable that muckrakers who only target their audience as the urban middle class or an elite segment within it have failed to realize the full potential of muckraking.[8]

Muckraking has been associated with many traditions in twentieth-century America. Most commentators emphasize the intimate connection between muckraking journalism and American liberalism. Indeed, many, if not most, muckrakers have shared in the liberal tradition, found their best voice in liberal publications, identified theirs as liberal goals, and been treated as liberals by their audiences and students. But muckraking has not been exclusively connected to liberalism. Sinclair, Steffens, and some others, for example, identified themselves with ancient Judeo-Christian themes of prophecy and social justice. Others in the 1900s regarded themselves as heirs to such nineteenth-century reformers as the abolitionists. And a number of muckrakers today, including several represented in the final chapter of this book, prefer to think of themselves as reporters devoted to a general public interest but to no earlier tradition.

Despite its predominant connection to liberalism, muckraking journalism has also converged on occasion with the issues and usages of both American conservatives and American radicals. A number of important early muckrakers, including John Spargo, Charles Edward Russell, and Upton Sinclair, reflected their Socialism in their works. Others, including Steffens and Baker, flirted with and praised the Socialists. I.F. Stone and those connected with *Hard Times* and *Ramparts* in recent times have muckraked for their respective versions of radical change. Stone regards Sinclair's ideas as an important influence on his own journalism. The value of muckraking for conservatism has rarely been recognized because of conservatives' usual antagonism to muckraking. James B. Dill, a major promoter of trusts, quietly provided Steffens with material to attack certain monopoly arrangements for many years. Samuel Hopkins Adams' muckraking series on patent medicines was reprinted and given a half-million-copy distribution by the American Medical Association. The New

York Stock Exchange, the Chicago Board of Trade, and individual financiers before 1907 endorsed and helped muckraking journalists so long as their attacks were being launched against "bucket shops" and a few other embarrassing Wall Street practices.[9]

Muckraking has a ticklish association with the commercial needs of the media in which it normally appears. To profit from advertising dollars, to build and maintain audience acceptance, and simultaneously to advocate social change is a formula for conflict. The *American Magazine*, partly owned after 1906 by muckrakers who wrote for it, saved itself from economic foundering by casting overboard its muckraking.[10] Some muckrakers turned to the partisan press, such as the privately subsidized *Nation* and *New Republic*, or like Sinclair published their own writings to bypass media barriers against controversial views. Interestingly, it was money making, some have charged, that caused the *Saturday Evening Post* and *Life* in their waning years and certain magazines copying *McClure's* early in this century to *add* muckraking to their usual pursuits. These media are alleged to have provided a kind of muckraking which entertained and reinforced audience attitudes—the usual service of popular journalism—in order to demonstrate to advertisers their appeal to a middle-class buying public suddenly "ready" for muckraking. Their subsequent investigations allegedly focused on "safe" topics, guaranteed to arouse indignation, such as trusts, organized crime, or pollution, without assigning specific responsibility or proposing harsh remedies. Like the blockbuster novels discussed in this book by John Cawelti, such muckraking journalism becomes a version of "inside dopesterism," loses its element of protest, and ends captive to mass entertainment and all the passing moods on which it seizes. Finally, after any noticeable shift in the winds of public attitudes, it is abandoned.

Not so, say proponents of muckraking who are alive to the dangers of advertiser pressure and audience fickleness. Advertisers and audiences are more quickly lost than gained by muckraking in the mass media. Muckraking by such licensed media as television raises additional threats of control by Congress, the White House, the F.C.C., and organized pressure groups. Just as small profits and small audiences do not attest to effective muckraking, they argue, neither does a mass audience for muckraking indicate a necessary dilution of investigation and exposure. Praise must be accorded the public which forces the big-audience media to direct their attention to real social needs. And who could be opposed to a responsive mass public for muckraking?

Muckraking has proved its ability to pierce the conscience of Americans. It has played and continues to play many roles within the American press and society. The aspects of muckraking probed in the following pages do not begin to exhaust its complexity or its worth to the American people.

Notes

1. *The New York Times,* March 24, 1968; Larry L. King, "Confessions of a White Racist," *Harper's Magazine,* 240 (Jan. 1970), 74; Orrin E. Clapp, *Heroes, Villains and Fools* (Englewood Cliffs, N.J., 1962), p. 54. Also consider Jack Anderson's "Merry-Go-Round" column of Aug. 8, 1970, in which he reported that a Washington concern will sell a "new muckracking service" to political candidates who want "political dirt" on opponents.

2. Stephen Donadio, "Columbia: Seven Interviews," *Partisan Review,* 35 (Summer 1968), 380–81; Daniel P. Moynihan, "The Presidency & the Press," *Commentary,* 41 (March 1971), 42.

3. John L. Spivack, *A Man and His Times* (New York, 1967), pp. 396–438.

4. Glenn Frank, *An American Looks at His World* (Newark, Del., 1923), p. 61; James Rorty, "The Post-War Social Mind," in *American Labor Dynamics in the Light of Post-War Developments,* ed. J.B.S. Hardman (New York, 1928), p. 78; Lincoln Steffens, "As Steffens Sees It," *The Survey Graphic,* 68 (Oct. 1, 1931), 12–14; *The Christian Science Monitor,* Mar. 14, 1963; James Harvey Young, *The Medical Messiahs* (Princeton, N.J., 1967), pp. 162–63.

5. Charles Peters and Taylor Branch, eds., *Blowing the Whistle* (New York, 1972), p. 3.

6. *Blowing the Whistle,* p. 4.

7. Walter Lippmann, *Drift and Mastery* (Englewood Cliffs, N.J., 1961 reprint), pp. 24–25.

8. See the editors' introduction to chap. 2.

9. Judson Grenier, "Upton Sinclair and the Press: *The Brass Check* Reconsidered," *Journalism Quarterly,* 49 (Autumn 1972), 427; Harry Stein, "Lincoln Steffens: Interviewer," *Journalism Quarterly,* 46 (Winter 1969), 735–36; James H. Cassedy, "Muckraking and Medicine: Samuel Hopkins Adams," *American Quarterly,* 16 (Spring 1964), 86; Cedric B. Cowing, *Populists, Plungers and Progressives* (Princeton, N.J., 1965), pp. 29–30, 38.

10. John E. Semonche, "The *American Magazine* of 1906–1915: Principle vs. Profit," *Journalism Quarterly,* 40 (Winter 1963), 36–44.

The preeminent historian of muckraking asks, "What of their work merits attention today?" and responds that in their active faith in a public interest and in their quest for a "valid society," less for their relationship to particular social problems and issues, the muckrakers of the Roosevelt and Taft years deserve emulation. Their substantive accomplishments seem to Louis Filler limited and dated yet historically interesting, a token of the moderate, respectable concerns of the middle-class public which called muckraking into being, chose democratically from its survey of social resources and opportunities, and within a dozen years allowed muckraking to decline as a change-maker. To judge muckraking, historians must also judge the American public and its shifting support for liberal reform. Restoration of muckraking authority in the 1970s, if it is to occur, appears to Filler dependent on accepting a new vocabulary and shape in the media, on new programs and public needs, and on maintaining, never denigrating, its ties to the middle class and middle-class virtues.

The author raises many more provocative issues than he can develop in a short paper. Respectful of the diversity of the early muckrakers, he urges evaluation of their art, not just their exposes, a task taken up in chapters 5 and 6 by John Cawelti and Jay Martin. By assuming that muckrakers practiced their faith in a "public interest," Filler ignores the possibility that such a doctrine, in itself, may have prevented early muckrakers from appreciating subcultures, as David Chalmers indicates (chapter 4), with contrary (or no) definitions of the public interest. The "public interest" in a nation of minorities may be a meaningless abstraction clothed with popular social authority to hurt rather than help a heterogeneous people.

Filler may also overestimate muckraking's dependence on an admittedly fickle middle class and the profit-making media which serve it. Muckraking may have elicited a less articulate, though still valuable, reception from other than middle-class publics. The muckraking newsletter *In Fact*, George Seldes remembers in *Never Tire of Protesting*, enjoyed a healthy circulation among C.I.O. union members from 1940 to 1948. In earlier years, Benjamin B. Lindsey received frequent praise from working-class readers for his muckraking of crime and juvenile delinquency, according to Charles Larsen's *The Good Fight*. Until muckraking by newspapers has been more extensively studied, the mass audience attentive to political exposures by the Chicago *Daily News* and the St. Louis

Post-Dispatch will be unappreciated. So, too, the mass popularity accorded the syndicated "Washington Merry-Go-Round" column since the 1930s. Little is known of the nature, depth, or direction of youth interest in *Ramparts* and the recent muckraking by some underground newspapers. There may always have been sufficient support among those of a non-middle-class life style or radical politics to maintain a number of unique muckraking publications and series. The related view, though not voiced by Filler, that muckrakers never have found much welcome in rural or small-town America has also been stated without real evidence. As Filler indicates, muckraking journalism cannot be understood if only the stated intentions and alleged motivations of its practitioners are studied and not their audience as well.

The Muckrakers and Middle America

Louis Filler

It is not human or even reasonable to treat a great social phenomenon of the past without in some sense, directly or otherwise, considering its relationship to the present. In the case of muckraking it is impossible to ignore the modern implications. For muckraking is a living phenomenon. Writers claim they are muckrakers. Publications, and not of the *True* or *Fact* variety, ask credit for muckraking. One might well wonder what caused seemly magazines like *Life*, with much to lose and a need for the patronage of great conservative businesses, to think muckraking would coin revenue for them and augment their readership.

To be sure, there are those today who do not love muckraking. *Barron's Magazine* thinks it is unfair to business and its leaders, and that it irresponsibly shakes public confidence in our social and economic order. Important public officials, who have been "exposed" by enterprising reporters, denounce "muckraking" journalists and mean by that lying and unfair journalists. So muckraking's two old reputations—of significant exposure without fear or favor, on one side, and of shabby and malicious rumor-mongering, on the other—both continue in the present as in the past. We might well look over those two reputations and decide what we think of them today. Doing so could tell us something about our national character, and its permutations over the years.

Most of us will suspect that muckraking, though it exploded on the scene unexpectedly and without a name, shortly after the twentieth century began, must have had precedents. Certainly there was public corruption. There were public figures caught in awkward postures. Alexander Hamilton was early accused by Jeffersonians of tipping off his gentlemen associates of fortune and good birth that the Federal government intended to fund the public debt and pay off speculators in Continental currency. Whigs thundered when Andrew Jackson stalwart Samuel Swartwout ran off to Europe with what remained of a million and a quarter dollars of public money. Abolitionists exposed the effort to get Texas into the Union as a plot by pro-slaveholders and the holders of Texas scrip.

Corruption highlighted the era of Grant, and the Tweed Ring, and inspired criticism and analysis. Yet we find something different from muckraking about these periods of public expose, not entirely clarified by the fact that they were partisan-inspired. Federalists versus Jeffersonians, Democrats versus Whigs, Republicans versus Democrats—naturally they "exposed" one another; but whether or how much the public weal gained from the exposes remains to be seen.

Thus, the New York *Times* in 1871 led the fight against Tweed and his minions in New York; but did it do so because of its hatred of official crime or because of its hatred of Democrats? The Republican *Times* was not a leader in exposing the crimes of Grant's minions in government. Elmer Davis, in his history of the *Times*, delicately noted that "[t]o the scandals which flourished in Washington . . . the editors of the *Times* could not be blind; . . . though their Republican principles made them sometimes delay . . . condemnation rather too long in the hope that the party would do its own housecleaning." Nevertheless, the *Times* ardently supported Grant for a second term while reprobating his opponent, Horace Greeley, as spokesman for an "unprincipled gang."[1]

So, though New York was well rid of Tweed, the *Times* campaign does not shine out of the past as muckraking. It was simply part of the competition and easy ethics of its particular time. A disillusioned generation like ours looks skeptically behind deeds to motives and, outside of partisan commitments, gives honor in small doses, and grudgingly. It can even be critical of those forces which unseated Tweed, as in one study which sees the Tammany chieftain as a "master communicator," and one who "with a fresher hand . . . rallied diverse groups behind his programs." The contrast here is with the Council of Political Reform which took over from Tweed's wrecked regime, and which widened the distance between itself and the poor and foreign of the city, in the process sacrificing every type of social improvement.[2]

Thus, any attack on crime and skulduggery can become outmoded, and leave no residue of honor to the reformer. Fighting the rich as opposed to the poor may prove little. The poor can prove "reactionary," as can the rich. The rich have subsidized revolution; Joseph Fels, of Fels-Naptha

Soap, provided the loan which enabled Lenin, Trotsky, Stalin, and others of the Fifth Congress of the Russian Social Democratic Party to continue their revolutionary debates in London in 1907.[3] Mabel Dodge Luhan's famous New York salon of the 1910s welcomed and was attentive to the revolutionary slogans of "Big Bill" Haywood. And so in still later decades. Muckraking virtue, by itself, will no more save it from forgetfulness than it did George Jones of the New York *Times*, whose persistence helped dethrone Boss Tweed.

Partisanship is not confined to Democrats and Republicans. We are all partisans on some issues. And yet there is something which can be defined as the public weal, in which we all have a stake. The most individualistic and special-interest group among us wants law and order of some kind, and appeals to questions of right and wrong. These terms change their targets to some extent, but the quest for a valid society goes on. The pre-muckraking era had its heroes and villains, its conservatives and reformers. It had some quasi-"muckraking" productions, such as the Adamses' *Chapters of Erie* (1871), which dealt with the lurid railroad frauds of the time, and Henry Demarest Lloyd's *Wealth Against Commonwealth* (1894), which muckraked Standard Oil. The sufferings of underpaid workers and of the unemployed were easily discerned during those years of little welfare and no security, and drew the attention of journalists and humanitarians. Their sympathy affected readers, and furthered the separate drives of trade unionists, of Populists, of Single Taxers, of socialists, and others.

And yet, to repeat, muckraking, when it came, was new. It created a new style and new goals, for better or worse, and our modern neomuckrakers have them in mind, rather than Ignatius Donnelly or Edward Bellamy, Frank Parsons or Henry George, Jacob A. Riis or Helen Hunt Jackson. What was it that distinguished the muckrakers from their humanitarian, or otherwise public-spirited, predecessors?

Hardly a muckraker had any expectation of becoming a muckraker. Charles Edward Russell, who emerged as the most single-minded, the most dedicated of the muckrakers, had just retired from journalism to write on poetry and similar matters when, as he said, he found himself with a muck rake in his hand. True, Russell's western Populist background prepared him for a career in civic concerns. But his spirit was not that of a politician or publicist; it was that of an artist or orator, of one who felt himself responsible for the quality of life, rather than merely for the state of an industry or of an administration. It is important to understand this distinction, for an assessment of muckraking will ultimately have to deal with it. The muckrakers not only wrote exposes. They also wrote novels and poems. And while we must weigh the accuracy of their exposes, it may also be necessary to give attention to their art. We may ultimately find that it is not for their accuracy that one or another of them may be memorable or useful to us today. It could be that their approach to life is at least as important to us as their articles or art. We read to learn, but we read, also, to emulate.

Other muckrakers were drawn out of circumstances similar to these of Russell. They were midwesterners or westerners—a significant percentage of them were that—who came to the big cities to become journalists and to find out what the new world created by Darwin's vision and industry's technology was all about. Many of them burned to write fiction, that is, to generalize their views of life. Receiving little encouragement from the elite publications—*Harper's, Century, Forum,* and others—they turned to journalism, where they could earn their bread and study their changing society. Some of them were turned into cynics or pessimists by their newspaper experiences. Theodore Dreiser, frequently misconstrued to have been a muckraker, exemplified these stormy characters. But those who survived their disillusionments, like David Graham Phillips, expressed a positive view which said that though there was evil in life, life could be controlled, through knowledge, and goodwill, and public debate.

Though the bulk of the muckrakers were journalists, skillful in dealing with particular issues which engaged their generation, and with a powerful ability to popularize complex issues, they were nevertheless varied in purposes and abilities. Thus, Russell was indeed a journalist who gathered data to expose industrial chicanery, churches as corporations, the evils of prison life, and other issues which finally made a socialist of him. But Upton Sinclair, though also capable of journalism, was a person of different substance. He had written pulp stories and dreamed of poetry in the vein of Heine and Shelley before he found himself in Chicago's Packingtown and emerged with the novel of that generation. Jack London was yet a different sort; a lawless boy who fought his way out of a raw, fatherless youth to preach primitive instinct as courage, but also to decry exploitation and, in a welter of personal contradictions, to stand up for the socialism of his time. Alfred Henry Lewis was, once again, different. I mention him only because he is, for general purposes, unknown, except as an alleged western humorist and author of the famous Wolfville stories. Lewis was a genius, but, unfortunately for neat categories, he also rated as a muckraker, though his shoddy contributions to expose only serve to muddle an easily muddled field.

Muckraking is, of course, most conveniently approached not through such figures as these, but through *McClure's Magazine* and the immortal combination of Lincoln Steffens, Ida M. Tarbell, and Ray Stannard Baker. Not much can be done about this, though they are sufficiently qualified by Sinclair, and the Phillips of *The Treason of the Senate*, and the Finley Peter Dunne of *Mr. Dooley* fame, to suggest more complexity than do by themselves *The Shame of the Cities*, *The History of the Standard Oil Company*, and Baker's presently most conspicuous title, *Following the Color Line*. *McClure's* was certainly a great muckraking magazine, but it cannot by itself carry the weight of muckraking, or tell us what muckraking was.

For one thing, muckraking was a development. In 1901 it was unknown. By 1903 it had been discovered, and in another year was shaking the nation's magazine journalism with revelations and challenges. It activated not only newspapermen, but also progressive politicians, social workers, municipal reformers, and such financiers as Thomas W. Lawson, who, for his own reasons, was ready to turn upon his associates in the interests of a more equitable commerce.

Muckraking accreted new partisans and lost old ones. It lost, for example, Herbert N. Casson, who in 1901 was a brilliant young critic of capitalism and a proponent of socialism, and who after 1907 was writing of the romance of steel, of the McCormick Reaper, the Bell Telephone system, and other industrial phenomena. Now it is possible to argue that Casson had not abandoned his earlier ideals, but had learned new ones. It is also possible, in rebuttal, to insist that his brave new histories and interpretations were shallow and unmemorable.

It must, however, also be recalled that the most dedicated of the muckrakers have themselves been accused of shallowness and mere sensationalism. Russell is substantially forgotten; nothing by him is in print. Phillips is waved off as a hasty journalist and poor novelist, no attention of any sort being accorded by literary critics to such of his admirers as Ludwig Lewisohn, Frank Harris, and the earlier H.L. Mencken. Tarbell and Baker are mere names to the general reader. Finley Peter Dunne is better remembered, or at least respected; and Lincoln Steffens's *Autobiography* is healthily in print. But how much their individual prose affects our regard for their muckraking heyday is yet to be determined.

It is, therefore, not sufficient to give lip service to the exposes of muckraking, or even to such of its achievements as the life-insurance investigations of 1905–6 or the Pure Food and Drug Act of the latter years. Both of these are obviously outdated. Any honor we accord them must be historical. If anything remains of their glory, it must inhere in the quality of their achievement, which, presumably, we are free to imitate.

The main drive of exposure, and of positive programs which muckrakers and progressives developed, was thought to be the rescue of the individual and the curbing of the corporations. Yet it is on precisely this issue that the muckrakers have been challenged, as in Gabriel Kolko's *The Triumph of Conservatism* (1963). This thoughtful study argues that the corporations were far from hating government intervention in their affairs. On the contrary, they needed it for their own well-being. Robber-baron free enterprise shook public confidence and made uniform control of prices and production difficult. Industry could best serve itself through government regulation, government law. So the muckrakers, by demanding federal agencies to oversee the operations of business were not aiding true free enterprise, but helping to bury it. The famous suits against the American Tobacco Company and the Standard Oil Company were not the great blows against monopoly of which President William Howard Taft boasted. They merely initiated a regulatory process which helped stabilize the industries and more efficiently define their power structures.

It is hard to disagree with Kolko's analysis, but its implications are less clear. Ida Tarbell, for example, had never denied that Standard Oil *was* a great corporation, and that the efficiency it sought *was* desirable. Her quarrel was with its methods, which had condoned the illegal crushing of competitors, and its ability to rig prices and business conditions to suit its purposes first and the public good second. And so with other, and more militant muckrakers. They were not opposed to business; Russell termed it, "the heart of the nation." They were opposed to business, as they saw it, which did not sufficiently benefit the public.[4]

As we have seen, there were muckrakers of every hue. Harvey W. Wiley, a chemist with a muckraking flair, wanted unadulterated food. Will Irwin wanted honest, one might say unadulterated, news. Upton Sinclair, of course, denied that it was possible to get either without socialism, but the fact was that both Dr. Wiley and Will Irwin had published their exposes for the general public. The public had it in its hand to vote them either up or down. What did it want? One thing can be clearly stated. The public did not want socialism, at least in the form in which it was currently being offered.

Seen from this perspective, the muckraking era was, in effect, one in which the public was being given a survey of its choices and resources, and asked where it did wish to go. The range of exposes was broad. It included bad housing, and other municipal problems; prostitution, gambling, and drink, among other patently moral issues; the state of politics and the state of religion; industry, labor, and the condition of women and children. Thus, the reading public, through such publications as *McClure's*, *Everybody's*, *Success*, *Collier's*, the *American Magazine*, and *Hampton's*, among others, and implemented by such moderate organs as the *Saturday Evening Post* and the *Ladies' Home Journal*, which pushed more limited campaigns—the reading public could in effect assert its interests and its preferences among causes.

If one prepares a graph of those preferences, he discovers what at bottom concerned that great reading public. It was faced with profound labor problems, but unwilling to probe too deeply into them. The crucial trial of "Big Bill" Haywood and other leaders of the Western Federation of Miners charged with the murder of ex-Governor Frank Steunenberg of Idaho resulted in acquittal. But the public which followed that trial gave relatively little attention to the equally significant *Danbury Hatters* 1908 United States Supreme Court decision, which put a crushing burden of fines on an embattled union for having instituted a secondary boycott against anti-union hat manufacturers. The public was only partially pro-labor. It was only partially interested in muckraking of its leading financial citizens. Gustavus Myers's *History of the Great American Fortunes*, a storehouse of fact concerning the harsh methods by which these fortunes were accumulated, was ten years without a publisher, and then was issued in 1909–10 only by a socialist publishing house. Though there were close to a million socialist votes in the 1912 election, Myers's *History* sold relatively little. Even socialists did not want this socialist arsenal of facts which downgraded American free enterprise.

The general public was only partially interested in regulating the stock market, and in regulating banks; it was willing to take a chance in hope of profit. It would take the 1929 market crash to achieve regulation of sorts in these fields. The public was only partially interested in women and children who worked in the factories. It would take the hideous Triangle Shirtwaist Co. fire of 1911, with its several hundred charred young women, to initiate useful legislation providing for factory inspection. But only to initiate. And a child-labor law would be struck down by the Supreme Court in 1918, and again in 1922. Child labor would also have to be taken care of by the 1929 crash, after which grown men—unemployed and desperate—would compete with their children for jobs of any kind.

What, then, did Americans of the 1900's demand, as a result of a torrent of exposes and investigations? Pure food and drug regulation, of course. A somewhat better-controlled insurance industry than had grown up under the sharp and often inhumane circumstances of private industry. And a railroad-regulation act which put government modestly into the business of helping to decide how much public responsibility the railroads —and, ultimately, other businesses—had to their vast and dependent publics.

After a decade of muckraking, the public continued to find itself uninterested in greater control of industry than a Department of Commerce, a Federal Trade Commission, and a Department of Labor could maintain. It continued to think the tariff issue important, and held it against Taft and his Republican Party that they had not carried out promises to scale the tariff downward. It continued an interest in currency manipulation—thanks in part to its painful experience with the Panic of 1907— only to the extent of approving a Federal Reserve Bank.

The public's interest in foreign affairs, in peace, and in international cooperation was minimal throughout the Progressive era. The public was not offended by Roosevelt's Big Stick policies. It did not protest the accession of the Panama Canal, Dollar Diplomacy, Big Navy perspectives, or any other of the appurtenances of imperialism. Some of the muckrakers were anti-imperialist in perspective. Hamilton Holt of the *Independent Magazine* was tireless in his search for peace. Charles Edward Russell was outstanding in his search for democracy abroad; his humane reputation would rebound upon him during World War I, when he took his stand against what he called "Junkerism," and endorsed President Wilson's European Crusade. During the muckraking era, in any case, neither the muckrakers nor their public made a significant target of militarism or held it against Roosevelt or Taft that they had approved the crushing of the Filipino Insurrectionists.

Conservation the Progressives did approve, and made of it one of the most brilliant of the muckraking causes, during the so-called Ballinger affair when, it was alleged, holdings in Alaska of great potential were secretly plotted to be removed from the public domain. Conservation was a major cause during the muckraking era and one of its heritages to the future, later reactivated during the Teapot Dome affair, and in still later campaigns involving water power, other natural resources, and, more recently, pollution.

In addition, there were adjuncts to muckraking which are not generally appreciated. Thus, the N.A.A.C.P. was born in that era—not a direct accomplishment of muckraking, but inconceivable without its more general appeal to human rights, and the direct aid of such partisans of the time as the white Oswald Garrison Villard and numerous other journalists and social workers. Similarly, other minorities received increased aid in education, union organization, and public sympathy and understanding, thanks to the writings of muckrakers.

Still, it adds up a relatively meager record of accomplishment, if one compares the era with the urgent needs of health, education, welfare, civil rights, minority problems, and sound planning on local, state, and national levels, to say nothing of the dreadful problems in foreign affairs which were soon to reduce much of Progressivism to an incinerated heap of lost hopes and outmoded language and ideals.

Add to the muckraking achievements, if you will, those of the Woodrow Wilson administration, with its loans to farmers, labor's Magna Carta (the Clayton Act), the seaman's Magna Carta (the La Follette Act), railroad mediation, the Underwood Free Trade Act, and others. We are still left with a meager harvest of regulation and deeds.

And, finally, put this record against a new, bitter sophistication, fed by the Marxism spawned by the Bolshevik Revolution and the revelations of Sigmund Freud. We would seem to put muckraking back, back in history: farther back than movements which it superceded: movements of revolution and of abolition—movements which seem, in the language of Thomas Paine and of Wendell Phillips, to speak more ringingly to the future than ever David Graham Phillips or Upton Sinclair, to say nothing of Lincoln Steffens, could speak. After all, it was Steffens who, as the ironist of the post-World War I era, advised the then-communist Whittaker Chambers to pay no attention to the reformers of his own generation.[5]

What is at stake here is our estimate of the American middle class— what we now call Middle America. For it was to it that the muckrakers spoke so successfully in the first decade of our century. It was the Populist, rural America, retooled for the twentieth century, and proliferating social activists by the thousands who presumed to lay down guidelines for future American development. Activists like Jane Addams, Homer Folks,

Robert Hunter, Samuel Gompers, Florence Kelley. Activists like Edwin Markham, Louis D. Brandeis, Tom Johnson, Brand Whitlock, W.E.B. Du Bois, Edgar Gardner Murphy. Activists like Benjamin B. Lindsey, E.A. Filene, and as many more as patience will attend to. These progressives offered particular programs for their own time. But more importantly, they presumed to offer *a method of approach* to American problems. And it is this method which, for better or worse, will be their tombstone or immortality.

They liked to quote De Tocqueville, to the effect that the cure for the ills of democracy was more democracy. They believed in the people— that same people which patronized Charles Sheldon's silly social fiction, James Whitcomb Riley's verse, and Billy Sunday's evangelism. Herbert Croly, soon to be the editor of *The New Republic*, scorned the muckrakers as sentimentalists. So did Woodrow Wilson, then the proud president of Princeton University. The muckrakers lacked insight, these intellectuals believed. The people, in fact, needed to be administered by their best, not by their most representative. And, in the 1910s, the muckrakers went down. It is popular to imagine that a kind of conspiracy took their magazines away from them, but if it did, the "conspiracy" included more than bankers. The banks, it is true, had once gladly lent the muckrakers money for profitable journalistic enterprises; they now called in their short-term loans, and in other ways stopped their publications. But Croly was unmoved by the muckrakers' demise, and he and his cohorts did nothing to prevent it. Similarly, it may be noted, the *Saturday Evening Post* in our own time, fighting desperately with muckraking weapons to stay afloat, went down a multimillion-dollar maelstrom. It is foolish to imagine that common skulduggery of the type routinely utilized in every business and institution in the country accounted for this phenomenon. It was a public judgment, not a private judgment which determined the result. The leader of the muckraking movement on the *Saturday Evening Post*, Clay Blair, holds that muckraking defeated him; that the public wanted sweetness and light; as he says:

> I think if I had it to do over again, I would keep Norman Rockwell on the cover. I wouldn't muckrake. I would try to find the things in America that are beautiful and good. In other words, the positive aspects of our society. I wanted to expose everything. I thought our society was on the brink of collapse, and I wanted to point out all the flaws. But in terms of magazines, the big ones, I think the people are damn sick and tired of trouble, trouble, trouble. You get it every night

on Huntley-Brinkley and Walter Cronkite. You get the war right in your living room and you see riots on the campus and riots in the ghettos. I think, my God, how much of this can you take? I don't have to be reminded of these things. Old Ben Hibbs' escapist concept might not be bad.[6] 1970

Perhaps. For the moment, it may suffice that the public which originally called muckraking into being decided to abandon it. In the 1910s, it demanded a modified *Collier's*, a modified *Saturday Evening Post*, a modified *McClure's*—magazines which we tend to call "merely entertainment," and whose art we derogate. But its original art was also derogated—the fiction of David Graham Phillips, the verse of Edwin Markham —so this would not be news.

In the end, the reading public, though it had been taught by muckrakers that there was evil in the world—that financiers were untrustworthy counselors, that resources would dwindle if they were not better policed, that the poor and helpless would suffer and the cities deteriorate if municipal arts were not advanced—the public decided to endorse a minimum of controls, and to leave progress to the skills of efficiency experts, radicals, and reformers: not, on the face of it, a bad combination.

The problem is with the equation. How efficient are the efficiency experts? How competent are the radicals and reformers? To be sure, World War I committed the nation beyond peacetime premises. It created internal hatreds and disappointments which complicated the problem of picking up causes of social betterment and carrying them to new ground.

But this situation was not really new. We have always had to work within the confines of our human nature. Especially in a land of minorities, questions of justice and injustice abound. Our problem is to forge new programs out of old, allowing for changing times and for changing vocabularies. Our problem is not to demand more of old crusaders than we ask of ourselves.

This is not the place to discuss the changing equations of reform and radicalism which developed in the 1920s and the 1930s, and beyond. It does have to be noted that the premises and means created in that period differed from those of the earlier crusaders. Muckrakers were certainly an elite, but part of their function had been to study the reading masses and to minister to their needs. The new elite of the twenties and thirties feared the masses, and continued to minister for them, rather than to them. To be sure, communist skulduggery could be substantially distinguished from New Deal rhetoric. But both despised Babbitt and the booboisie. Both decried parochialism and praised expatriates and internationalists. The muckrakers had once identified themselves with American traditions, American loyalties; they had identified patriotism with reform. The new reformers scorned patriotism as the conviction of morons and identified flag-waving with vigilantes, prohibitionists, and others who constricted individual rights.

All of this, perhaps, describes a tragedy at least as much as a conspiracy. The outlines of both may be discerned in such writings as George Seldes's *Tell the Truth and Run* (1958), Benjamin Gitlow's *The Whole of Their Lives* (1948), and Murray Kempton's *Part of Our Time* (1955), and yet to be judiciously examined, such writings by John Dos Passos as *Adventures of a Young Man* (1939) and *The Grand Design* (1949). And, in addition, it should be recalled that the new wave of reform and radicalism could claim such distinguished literary and social figures as John Dos Passos, John Howard Lawson, Kenneth Fearing, John Chamberlain, Richard M. Rovere, Granville Hicks, Clifford Odets, Arthur M. Schlesinger, Jr., Edmund Wilson, John Steinbeck, and Malcolm Cowley. It could claim the collaboration of scores of others, from Theodore Dreiser to Ernest Hemingway. Some of the new reformers and radicals had, too, a direct line with muckraking through such figures as John L. Spivak and I.F. Stone. Nevertheless, generally, artists could be distinguished from social activists somewhat more certainly than in the era of the muckrakers when novels seemed a fit vehicle for social criticism.

As we enter into the 1970s, and reconsider our heritage of the twentieth century, a judgment on the muckrakers—what they were and what they have to offer us—must be made, directly or indirectly. No one person can presume to say what that verdict will be. On the face of it, our circumstances differ greatly from theirs. We cope with looser family ties and more experimental sexual attitudes, arguments over the legitimacy of drugs and the relevance of religion, and, of course, violent, mind-filling problems in minority relations and the uses of the past. A loose, experimental individualistic pose would seem much in order for such a fluid situation.

Yet there are countertendencies which some of us grasp at eagerly and others fear and reject: tendencies toward that much-controverted "law and order," toward control of crime, toward a damping of easy dissent, minority expression, and educational privilege.

Should protest pick up anew, we can expect that "old-fashioned virtues"

—the virtues which the muckrakers at least outwardly admired—may continue to lie in limbo. And since muckraking has been criticized as old-fashioned, unwilling or unable to get at the roots of trouble, and bad art, there should be no reason to disturb this judgment.

But there could be a recrudescence of fundamentalism, nationalistic feeling, and local and sectional power. Minorities could be left to their own devices, as with "benign neglect," and education tightened up to mean formal competence and acceptance of given standards. This happened in the 1930s when, despite social unrest and even violence, the educational establishment held fast. If this should happen again, classic forces favoring civil rights and humanitarianism might wish to appeal for a new mobilization of democratic-minded Americans and a new regard for old dissenters. They might also find new uses not merely for the muckrakers, but also for their methods and ideals.

For one thing, they might discover that the muckrakers were not quite such "squares" as they have imagined partisans of the Square Deal to be. Many of them were drinkers; several of them were very close to being drunkards. Their sexual experiences were somewhat wider than many have imagined. Their religious convictions were much less firm.

From this point of view, they might even be seen as hypocrites, but their friends would not accept this. We are all aware of the distance between the ideal and the real in ourselves, and in people and movements we admire. If the muckrakers should ever be widely admired again, it will be because we think we need them, not because we have suddenly ourselves become "old-fashioned Americans."

And if we should need them, it will be because we have concluded that we require a criticism of American life which is more positive in its regard for middle-class ideals than it has been in recent decades. After all, Babbitt was an incident in American life, not its norm. So were Harding and Coolidge. We find the history we want, and what we find gives the measure of us, as well as of itself. The muckrakers elected to visualize a typical American who was aggressive and ambitious—what we tend to call "only human"—but who also had his civic side: his pride in his environment, his race, his nation. To such an American they appealed not only in terms of dollars and cents, though they saw the virtue in money, but in the individual terms of representative Americans and representative situations.

And here we come to the crux of our inquiry. What of their work merits attention today? There is much to cite out of other reform movements:

speeches, poems, essays, even stories. Though great writers tend to be too big to confine within a reform movement, they reflect the troubles of their age, and bear upon them in one fashion or another.

The muckrakers are a more doubtful case. That they ought to be used more fully and more directly than they are, I am certain. Whether they will be, remains to be seen. We read something by Finley Peter Dunne. We read Steffens's *Autobiography*: not a strictly muckraking production, and patently richer than Steffens's *The Shame of the Cities*, his most famous title. David Graham Phillips's *The Treason of the Senate* is a phenomenon, having been published as a book sixty years after its original magazine publication. But most of the muckraking has been lost, and whether any part of it will yet be recaptured for modern use is undetermined.

But whatever may be the fate of the muckrakers' art, their *method* needs to be reconsidered. Was it wrong? Was the *Saturday Evening Post* recently misguided to think that its vast middle-class audience would be inspired by articles which revealed incompetence and bad faith on the part of public figures and symbols? Is it likely that we can pour our social time and energy into pornography and aimless euphoria, and still produce great movements leading to a reconstruction of our cities and of our lives?

And if we conclude that there can be no new and promising America without "middle America," then how do we approach it, how do we find common ground with it? Karl Marx once decried "rural idiocy" and saw it as the mission of the city-dwellers to free the provincials from their own inadequacies. We have lived long enough with the American city to know that there is such a thing as "urban idiocy" as well, and that a just approach will not prejudice one locale over another.

Our business is to distinguish the valid from the invalid whether it happens to reside in the city or in the suburbs. One is reminded of the scene in Benet's *The Devil and Daniel Webster* in which Webster as lawyer faces the infamous jury of cutthroats and traitors with hatred and indignation. They lean forward eagerly, their eyes glittering at him. Webster controls himself, as he realizes that his hatred will only call forth hatred. He must appeal to that in them that was good: their old, forgotten virtues of human pride, love of home, and love of people.

So we, if we scorn honesty as corny and patriotism as malignant, if we confuse simpleness with simplicity and religion with stupidity, then we will certainly attract the attention of corny, malignant, simple, and stupid people. The others will recede into that mysterious social equation which determines our national decisions—our best-sellers, our scandals, our political spokesmen, our courts, our educational standards—all the aspects of our affairs which go on whether we pay any attention to them or not. We are all aware that we follow and are influenced by different levels of attitude at one and the same time. We ponder T.S. Eliot and also Philip Roth. We worry about Vietnam and also about hemlines, about LSD, and about the high cost of living. Some people believe John V. Lindsay was reelected mayor of New York City because the Mets won the World Series.

We are wrong to think Middle America is out there waiting for us to respect it. It is no different from us in struggling for security, for dignity, for purpose. There are "cop-outs" in Middle America, just as there are in any other social sector. There always have been. The same majority silently watched the events in Selma, Alabama, several years back, and cast its psychological weight on them, as watched events in Berkeley, California, in Chicago on several momentous occasions, in Washington, and elsewhere. Is that silent majority interested in muckraking? Perhaps not. But it once was. And it could be again.

It has often been noted that we are Hamiltonians in good times, and Jeffersonians when trouble strikes. Nevertheless, even in the most affluent times there is likely to be a solid civil-rights and reformist interest, and not necessarily composed of poor and unfortunate people. A nation of upwardly mobile people and resentful poor can never rest, whether times are good or ill. It can forget formerly charismatic individuals with amazing rapidity, so much so that the same individual can often enjoy two opposing careers, one historical, the other current. It can forget issues overnight, turning from war and peace to pollution, for instance, even while a war continues. But it feels compelled to support a liberal establishment which, in the worst times for civil liberties, keeps fluid American traditions of freedom and license.

All of this does not necessarily redound to the benefit of a muckraking tradition, which was based on middle-class dialogue and the printed word. We do not always appreciate open forums, and we are not always willing to support them. It has been argued recently that it is not magazines which are in economic trouble, but the printed word, and in truth, television already has a historic record of having influenced public decisions. It has even exercised patent muckraking functions, as in past efforts by Mike Wallace and David Brinkley to turn headlights on key issues of violence and on corruption in road-building. It is not certain, however, that television can be a major avenue for the development of memorable muckrakers, in the sense that magazines once were. More likely, the pictorial power of television would have to implement the printed power of magazines, in a new social equation of writing and expose. The significant phase of Ralph Nader's crusade began in a television revelation of skulduggery in industry which won the general public's sympathy. Whether Mr. Nader foreshadows a new concern for the basics of American life, and whether writers will emerge on the old model to create new standards of social deportment and responsibility, cannot be known.

At the moment, our social services are in the hands of stipendiaries. There are on the scene no manifest Margaret Sangers, Gifford Pinchots, James Weldon Johnsons, Josephine Peabody Lowells, Thomas Mott Osbornes—individuals not only with competencies, but with dreams which truly imaginative writers could pass on to a reading and remembering public. At this time all this seems too remote from reality. We derive too much satisfaction from such writers as Jack Kerouac, Ernest Hemingway, John Cheever, Henry Miller, and Saul Bellow to develop a taste for more tradition-rooted scribes. Most likely we will meet our crises, if meet them we do, through specialized elite technicians, and leave our writing satisfactions to more individualistic elements and *tour de force* quasiradicals. David Graham Phillips once opined that the politician speaks with the lips of the people, the statesman with its heart. Tom Reed of the House of Representatives may have proved more correct in his view that the statesman is just a dead politician. Phillips's own career may be evidence that the will to serve may not be the capacity to serve. Service is a two-way arrangement.

But is Clay Blair correct in concluding that the American people want sweetness and light, Norman Rockwell, rather than muckraking? Is the choice between Norman Rockwell and Norman Mailer? One would think not. Van Wyck Brooks once offered the thought that Walt Whitman had precipitated the American character. Brooks meant that one could appeal to America's capacity for evil or its capacity for good. A full-blooded reform movement would not be concerned merely for equitable taxes or even better housing or purer air. It would be concerned for the meaning of life, of which temporary conveniences or inconveniences would be merely passing phases. We have all known patio communists and cocktail libertarians, and we are aware that something drains strength from their crusades. We recognize a wholeness about the lives of a William Lloyd Garrison or a Wendell Phillips such as we cannot readily pinpoint in many of our spiritual counselors. Our public—bingo and tv eyes and all—may be deeper than we think. They may understand us better than we realize. Our judgment of muckraking, then, is only partly a judgment of the public: its values and achievement. It is, in part, a judgment of ourselves. And it is this fact which gives weight and dimensions to our debates.

Notes

1. Elmer Davis, *History of the New York Times* (New York, 1921), p. 120.

2. Seymour J. Mandelbaum, *Boss Tweed's New York* (New York, 1956), pp. 70, 112–13.

3. Arthur P. Dudden and Theodore H. von Lau, "The RSDLP and Joseph Fels: A Study in Intercultural Contact," *American Historical Review*, 61 (1955), 21–47.

4. Charles Edward Russell, *Business: The Heart of the Nation* (New York, 1911).

5. Lincoln Steffens to Whittaker Chambers, June 18, 1933, in *The Letters of Lincoln Steffens* II, ed. Ella Winter and Granville Hicks (New York, 1938), p. 961.

6. "A Voice from the Grave," *New York*, January 12, 1970, p. 29.

PART III INTRODUCTION

Enlightened and educated opinion in the Progressive era was usually more socially advanced than that of the muckrakers about race relations and the delivery of justice in America. So say Robert Bannister, author of a notable biography of Ray Stannard Baker, and David Chalmers, author of *The Social and Political Ideas of the Muckrakers*. They differ, however, on whether muckraking exposes of the inadequate justice for black Americans led, rather than followed, this opinion. In a poisoned ideological atmosphere, Bannister concludes, muckraking suffered from the negative racial attitudes of most of its contributors and editors, their reluctance to offend reader sensibilities, a sometimes cruel willingness to underwrite racially negative audience values, and the muckrakers' unhappy acceptance of some denial of liberties as the price for social peace in the country. Bannister notes that some muckrakers nevertheless exposed the worst, if not all, racial evils of their day, and a few succeeded in moderating their own racial views. Their muckraking seems to have stimulated some action, sometimes quite different from what they had intended, at the local level, and to have had little impact on national policy.

Chalmers suggests that their journalism stirred far greater popular interest in urban corruption and other topics than in the problem of delivering justice in America. That system of justice delivery was little affected by muckraking, which tended toward superficiality of vision and of comment and lacked long-range commitment in treating events in the streets, police stations, courts, and prisons, he concludes. For experienced journalists they remained strangely ignorant of the salient subcultures of courts and other institutions which independently affected the quality of justice, and they overemphasized, Chalmers implies, that corruption and lawlessness in the delivery of justice were wholly equitable in cause and legislative solution to corruption and lawlessness in the market place. So, as Bannister and Chalmers variously propose, popular resistance and the muckraker's personal and professional limitations rendered muckraking an uncertain vehicle for changing the racial scene, and their particular defects in outlook and persistence hindered the muckrakers' arousing the public to altering the justice-delivery system.

The special virtues of Bannister's presentation are in his penetrating, heavily documented analysis and his serviceable questions and categories, such as those distinguishing between local and national influence. Chalmers, offering a more schematic appraisal, asks basically the same questions, and he vividly draws a connection between the *felt* manifestations of the justice-delivery problems today and in the years prior to World War I. Now, comparisons of the muckrakers' attitudes with the enlightened legal views and the content of the genteel magazines of that era should be supplemented by comparisons with the newspapers and mass-circulation, nonmuckraking periodicals of the same period and by examination of the private correspondence so revealing of motivation. Chalmers and Bannister acknowledge that the actual treatment of social problems and issues by the muckrakers constitutes a vital guide to the historical importance of such writings, and both are more skeptical than Filler of muckraking as a continuously effective vehicle for liberal reform. The three historians agree that muckrakers probably had more valuable, clearer, and more effective remarks on issues other than the justice system and race relations but that in retrospective judgment of the needs of the Progressive era, muckraking deserves a modest assessment.

It may be that muckrakers and those directing and printing their work in the Progressive era deserve a better appreciation. They had little or no control, as Bannister notes in particular instances, over the use made of their published writings. As journalists they expected and were required to move from place to place, topic to topic, without becoming experts; they had to popularize and be timely if they were to enjoy much influence, or even hold a job, and becoming highly knowledgeable about different subcultures was often impossible and could easily slide, endangering their autonomy as reporters. Nor should it be surprising that as journalists they were slower to suggest specific cures than to indicate conditions in need of remedy. It is a difficult task in any era to pierce the cover of ignorance or fatalism with words and images that make suffering concrete and indignities real to large numbers of Americans who consider themselves uninvolved. Muckrakers may sometimes induce and reflect widespread alarm and indignation and appear to move and shake one or another segment of opinion, authority, or institutional arrangement. They more often encounter a stony indifference or are faced by such oppressive hostility from powerful individuals and agencies that some of them abandon their activities or forsake hope of immediately bridging the gap between promise and possibility in America.

To the early muckrakers the lot of mankind often seemed at stake, and their labors were directed toward improving the quality of individual and social existence in the present with the tools of the present and the fond expectation that the momentum would continue. And meanwhile they guarded against abusing their own power, stigmatizing the weak and defenseless, assassinating the character of the prominent, or indulging in self-righteous gestures and moralistic posturing. To achieve credibility and avoid libel suits, they had to insist on a high level of accuracy and to temper their own outrage with a suggestion of pity, a dash of humor or irony, a measure of skepticism. That a few muckrakers softened in their racial attitudes, or that others, such as Lincoln Steffens and Ray Stannard Baker, achieved greater analytical depth in the process was a token of the great potential of muckraking for the media. So too muckraking helped balance and supplement the growing cult of objectivity and its tendency to transform intelligent and humane newsmen into voyeurs or frustrated cynics. Muckraking required imaginative thought about information in the writer's possession and lessened the danger of conveying only the half-truths or falsehoods which come of serving merely as a transmitter of other men's views. As analysis and communication, muckraking may be a segment of the social process through which a complex society differentiates between what is evil and what is socially good and legitimate. It may then be inevitable that muckraking in any era is destined to imperfect achievement and to be in dispute in the absence of consensus about what is criminal and evil. But whatever its failings, muckraking can never be dismissed as a labor without value to the United States and its people.

Race Relations and the Muckrakers

Robert C. Bannister, Jr.

During the Progressive era, many black Americans felt that the national press seriously ignored their grievances. "The magazines," charged the editor of the *Voice of the Negro*, "want to hold their southern subscribers and so they have thrown open their columns to the Vardamans and Dixons. When reply to such vile rot is submitted, the manuscript is returned with the statement that 'we do not care to open our columns to controversy'." When Theodore Roosevelt attacked the muckrakers, this same editor wished only that T.R. had scored the magazines for "muck-making" on the race issue. *The Crisis*, the journal of the NAACP, charged that *McClure's* had required Jane Addams to delete a paragraph criticizing the "lily-whitism" of the Bull Moosers. Another popular magazine allegedly commissioned an Englishman to study the race issue but, having paid him, suppressed the results when they proved too favorable to the Negro. Even the *Survey*, spokesman for more enlightened opinion among charity and settlement workers, required an author to omit a plea for equal social rights. By the end of the period it seemed that, as one black reader wrote to the muckraker Ray Stannard Baker, "the press has entered into a 'conspiracy of silence' on the wrong the nation is heaping upon the colored population."[1]

Several historians, questioning this indictment, have noted that whatever the policy of the press in general, the muckrakers made a considerable contribution to the cause of Negro rights. *McClure's*, *Cosmopolitan*, and the *American Magazine*, joining older journals like the *Independent*, *Nation*, and *Outlook*, denounced a rising tide of discrimination and violence. Ray Stannard Baker's *Following the Color Line* (1908) was an especially outstanding contribution. Thanks to their efforts, wrote one observer, "the Negro problem was taken out of the hands of reactionaries and scattered forces of well-wishing individuals and societies, and . . . raised to its rightful place among the most important social issues."[2]

Others have been more skeptical. "The Negroes," John Hope Franklin concluded, "could look neither to the White House nor to the muckrakers for substantial assistance." Not only were the contributions of the muckrakers few in number, but their efforts resounded with racial stereotypes now offensive to many whites. Even Baker's *Following the Color Line* has drawn criticism. Although generally praising the work, Gunnar Myrdal termed it a monument to the "static assumption" that benign neglect would best solve the race problem, an assumption Myrdal's *American Dilemma* (1944) explicitly challenged. The author of a study of the Atlanta riot of 1906, the event which triggered Baker's serious interest in the race problem, censured the reporter for failing to "transcend the racist assumptions of his era." Similarly, the author of a recent survey of "The Muckrakers and Negroes," while admitting that these journalists took "some serious interest" in the Negro, concluded that to have enlarged their "restricted" achievement would have required changes in attitude impossible for the pre-War generation.[3]

More generally, the question of the muckrakers and the race issue goes to the heart of recent charges that twentieth-century liberalism—the tradition of progressivism—has consistently ignored the interests of the urban and rural poor, especially the blacks, and is thus unable to provide solutions in the present crisis. That many pre-1914 liberals condoned new forms of discrimination seems abundantly clear.[4] Yet the question remains whether some groups with some success opposed the emerging consensus, thus tempering the reaction. The several dozen writers and editors who spearheaded muckraking,[5] because of their general contribution to progressivism, are especially significant in this connection. Sensitized by profession to public opinion, they provided one channel through which enlightened sentiment on the race issue might awaken an apathetic public. Their success, and the personal and institutional pressures that limited their efforts and their sympathies, provide valuable insight into the nature and promise of muckraking in the liberal reform tradition.

Concerning the muckrakers and race, three sorts of questions have been central. First, what precisely was their response, and how did it compare to discussions of race in the older journals? Second, in what ways did personal bias and/or editorial policy influence this response? Finally, insofar as one may speak of influence, what impact did the muckrakers have?

Although much of the interest and excitement of muckraking derives from alleged contrasts between a "new" and older journalism, it is easy to exaggerate the extent of this departure, especially on the race issue.[6] A number of journals, although limited in circulation in comparison with *McClure's* and the others, led in reporting racial injustice during the Progressive era. The religious press, in sheer quantity, was foremost. The *Independent*, edited by William Hayes Ward and Hamilton Holt, was the Negro's steadiest champion among national journals.[7] Not coincidentally, this journal published William English Walling's significant article on the Springfield riot of 1908, an account directly responsible for the formation of the NAACP.[8] The *Outlook*, edited by Lyman Abbott, also gave the race issue considerable space, but emerged finally as a spokesman for a brand of Rooseveltian equivocation which the NAACP branded "Bourbonism."[9]

The *Nation*, the *Arena*, and *Charities*, more exclusively concerned with politics and society, also focused the attention of their readers on the race issue. Although the *Nation*, since its founding in 1865, had diluted its initial devotion to absolute equality, it never entirely abandoned its early idealism. During the Progressive years it emerged as an outspoken critic of Jim Crow and disfranchisement.[10] The *Arena*, a radical journal edited by Benjamin Orange Flower, regularly included three or four articles a year (of sixty to seventy) on the race issue, some also critical of the emerging consensus.[11] *Charities*, which devoted an entire number to the race issue in 1905, thus provided a group discussion of the issue that was perhaps the most significant to appear in America to that date.[12]

Although the respectable monthlies often disseminated highbrow racism,[13] some gave the Negro sympathetic attention on occasion. The *Atlantic Monthly* and the *North American Review* in particular printed a number of articles that one black observer termed articles of "the greatest permanent value," a judgment reflecting their relatively balanced consideration of the Negro cause.[14] The *Atlantic*, concerned by the spread of disfranchisement laws, openly wondered what position should be adopted by "those who believe, as the *Atlantic* does, in the old-fashioned American doctrine of political equality, irrespective of race or color or station." To help its readers decide it ran during 1902 a series of thoughtful articles, one of which led to the forced resignation of its author, an Emory University professor, for its forthrightness.[15] The *Century* and *Harper's*, in contrast, gave the issue less space and generally deserve the criticism they have received. In 1903 Richard Watson Gilder of the *Century* refused the article by Carl Schurz which would subsequently launch *McClure's* into this area. In turning it down, Gilder revealed a policy of caution. "Your essay would probably be read more calmly in cooler weather," he urged, suggesting a delay. Finally he refused it outright, citing its excessive length. Although the usual *Century* article was shorter, the magazine's receptiveness to articles highly critical of the Negro indicates that more than length was involved.[16]

In sum, the muckrakers did not operate in a vacuum. When in 1903 Sam McClure launched the "literature of exposure" the race problem, like trusts and corruption, was not unknown. There had been and would continue to be sympathetic discussion of the issue, especially in smaller magazines which may be termed "muckrakers" only at the peril of considerable confusion. A nucleus of enlightened opinion existed. What was needed was a stark recitation of the mounting tide of discrimination in the style in which the new journalism excelled, and publicity that would carry the issue to a broader audience than the older periodicals served, awakening "Middle America."[17] The muckrakers, dramatizing injustice, might thus mobilize the public on an issue that white Americans rather preferred to forget.

A superficial look at the response suggests they met the challenge with characteristic boldness. *McClure's*, again the pioneer, led in January 1904 with a widely heralded discussion "Can the South Solve the Negro Problem" by Carl Schurz. Drawing on his experience in the post-Civil War period, Schurz condemned the reactionism that threatened the South with a new "peculiar institution" of semislavery. Attacking the new state constitutions, he insisted that disfranchisement by "direct or indirect" means was clearly in opposition to the Fifteenth Amendment. Although not muckraking in a strict sense, his article suited the mood of *McClure's*. What he offered, he admitted, was a "diagnosis" rather than a "definite remedy." What was needed was not more law or legal action (he purposely omitted reference to a popular proposal to punish the South by reducing representation) but a change in "public sentiment."[18]

Although many white southerners were outraged,[19] black leaders were pleased beyond measure. Booker Washington joined with DuBois and others to distribute reprints to the legislators and governors of all southern states, representatives of every branch of the federal government, and officials of all southern colleges. Reprints also appeared in *Liberia* and the African Methodist Episcopal *Church Review*. One Negro leader suggested that if the northern press generally were as brave as *McClure's*, "many of the abuses which bring such disgrace upon the Nation would be wiped out."[20]

During 1905, other contributions more clearly in the new genre appeared in both *McClure's* and *Cosmopolitan*, the latter purchased in 1905 by William Randolph Hearst. In *McClure's* Ray Stannard Baker, already acclaimed for his studies of the labor situation, initiated a two-part discussion of lynching. In *Cosmopolitan*, Herbert D. Ward, a popular novelist, attacked the peonage system. Neither writer presented solutions but rather documented the evils in crisp detail. The problem, Baker stressed, was lawlessness: the "only remedy," "a strict enforcement of the law, all along the line, all the time." Ward agreed. "We have laws enough," he wrote, "we need only an aroused public opinion and fearless officers to enforce these laws."[21]

The riot in Atlanta in the fall of 1906, like Watts and Detroit six decades later, triggered new interest. For the next two years the popular magazines looked more deeply than ever into the race question. The *American Magazine*, which Baker, Ida Tarbell, and others from the *McClure's* staff purchased in mid-1906, took the lead. An analysis of "The Negro Crisis" by the Social Gospeller Washington Gladden in January 1907 prefaced the appearance of Baker's *Following the Color Line*.[22] The *American* also published a steady stream of poems and stories which, however condescending in tone they may appear today, were designed to soften the hearts of middle-class whites.[23] In March 1907 *Cosmopolitan* renewed its attack on peonage in an article by a young California journalist, Richard Barry.[24] *Collier's*, which dabbled in muckraking, tried unsuccessfully to get Baker to do a series, and eventually published several sympathetic pieces which stood in marked contrast to the magazine's defense of Thomas Dixon and *The Clansman* in 1905.[25] *McClure's*, again judged only on the number of articles, continued to focus attention on the race question.[26]

By 1908 the muckraking crusade was changing character, and with it came a new phase in the discussion of race. Not content merely to arouse public opinion, individual muckrakers attempted to translate indignation into positive programs for change. Charles Edward Russell followed Upton Sinclair to socialism; and Lincoln Steffens had well begun the pilgrimage to radicalism he later described in his *Autobiography*. Baker, after also toying with radicalism, began to fashion a philosophy designed to resolve to his own satisfaction the growing tensions he perceived in American life, an enterprise he undertook simultaneously in his journalism and in the "Adventures in Contentment" he wrote under the pseudonym David Grayson.[27] These muckrakers also essayed solutions to the race problem. Baker, reversing his original intention to report only the facts, ended his *Following the Color Line* series with a statement of "Personal Conclusions."[28] Russell, for some time sympathetic to black aspirations, joined Lincoln Steffens in signing the "Call" that led to the formation of the NAACP.[29]

Meanwhile several new arrivals kept the muckraking spirit alive. Harris Dickson, a native southerner, contributed a series on the race issue to *Hampton's Magazine* in 1909. *Pearson's*, like *Hampton's* an heir of the original crusade, added several further discussions in 1910 and 1911. The *Twentieth Century*, successor to the *Arena*, published a sympathetic history of black writers. In another issue editor B.O. Flower wondered if the "caucasian cowardice" underlying lynching was "congenital."[30]

Indeed, from this superficial review, one might with some justice conclude that muckrakers gave the race issue national exposure, and to some degree opposed discrimination. Their response in fact followed the general pattern of the muckrake crusade: *McClure's* pioneered during the Roosevelt years; indignation yielded to more constructive analysis toward the end of the decade; and there occurred a brief revival between 1909 and 1912 in such magazines as *Hampton's* and *Pearson's*.

A closer look, however, raises problems requiring further analysis. Although the newer journals proved occasionally receptive to attacks on discrimination, the leading muckrakers, with a few exceptions, were remarkably silent. Steffens and Russell, whatever their personal views, barely mentioned Negroes in their published work. Most others ignored the issue entirely, publicly and privately, during the Progressive era and in their autobiographies.[31] Like other social issues race relations were primarily the province of what may be termed "special interest" contributors, many of whom differed in age or background from the typical muckraker. When Schurz's article appeared in *McClure's*, one reader noted that it was "refreshing to hear the fearless tones of the anti-slavery 'old guard',"[32] a characterization that equally fits others who preserved, in however fractured a form, something of the Civil War idealism: Oswald

G. Villard of the *Nation*; William Hayes Ward and Hamilton Holt of the *Independent*; Lyman Abbott of the *Outlook*.

Moreover, despite the articles cited above, *McClure's* and the others failed to make even the departures that distinguished their contributions from those of the older magazines on other issues. In range they were narrower, and in tone as unfavorable to the black cause as many articles in other periodicals. In the pure muckraking phase (as opposed to the extended analysis of *Following the Color Line*) the newer journals had essentially two concerns, lawlessness and corruption, primarily as evidenced in lynching and peonage, practices already widely condemned in both North and South. Idealistic impulses of idealism, while occasionally producing attacks on other forms of discrimination, characteristically yielded to support for a minimal reading of the Booker Washington program, or even to the sanction of segregation, colonization, or disfranchisement. To understand the forces that set these limits, it is necessary to weigh the impact of two crucial factors: the racial attitudes of the individuals involved, and the editorial policies of their magazines.

Although a great deal has been written concerning the racism of the Progressives,[33] the subject must be approached with caution. Few muckrakers underwrote the extreme pseudoscientific racism that I.A. Newby and others have described. If in some cases, outright or subterranean bias explained hostility or straddling, certain muckrakers partially transcended racial bias.

For some, perhaps many, a lack of contact with blacks bred simple indifference. As youths the muckrakers grew up in communities in which the black population was considerably less than 2%. In only one was it higher than 7%.[34] As adults, to judge from their published work, many remained ignorant of and indifferent to black America.

Innocence in other cases sustained a color blindness that combined idealism with naivete. William Allen White, the Kansas editor, sometime muckraker, and associate of Baker and Tarbell on the *American*, was truly repulsed by racial bias. Responding to a report that the University of Kansas was discriminating in its athletic facilities, he described prejudice as a "curious psychological mania" which, although personally unknown to him, was responsible, he had been told, for a "great deal of sorrow and injustice." During the 1920s, White battled the Ku Klux Klan in his native state.[35] Ida Tarbell, although less explicit in denouncing prejudice, also apparently assumed that simple justice required equal treatment for blacks.[36] Jacob Riis, who generally ignored the race issue, asserted that in twenty-five years of reporting in New York's "Old Africa" and other black districts he had seen no crime or other activity sufficiently peculiar to blacks to warrant mention by color.[37]

At the other extreme lay a racism of varying degrees. Both *Pearson's* and *Hampton's*, two magazines that rekindled muckraking after 1909, demonstrated how well racism fit the tested formulae of the new journalism. Side by side with revelations concerning corporate and political malfeasance, these journals "exposed" the dangers of racial amalgamation, black criminality, black political rule, and the "fallacies of the hysterical philanthropists and negrophiles."[38] The results were articles which, better even than those in *McClure's* or the *Cosmopolitan*, may be genuinely termed muckraking applied to the race issue. Their tone and rhetoric was early *McClure's*. "Facts" would allay a "fog of misunderstanding" bred by "sentimentalism and idealism," *Hampton's* proclaimed, introducing a series by the southerner, Harris Dickson. Replying to readers who condemned Dickson's overt racism, the editors noted they were "simply printing the plain, unvarnished truth that every American should know." *Pearson's*, summoning white Americans to their "responsibilities" in preserving "race purity," pronounced miscegenation "the real 'nigger' problem." The story of race mixture, "plainly told," was a "shocking revelation of the depravity of man."[39]

Although the earlier and more important muckraking magazines avoided such explicit appeals to racial fears, such were not entirely absent. Will Irwin, describing the "saloon evil" in *Collier's*, played on similar apprehensions in a controversial piece titled "Nigger Gin." Certain brands of cheap gin, picturing on their labels lewd pictures of white women, were directly responsible for race conflict and worse, he alleged. Imagining the gin an aphrodisiac, the ignorant southern black as Irwin described him, "sits in the road or in the alley at the height of his debauch, looking at that obscene picture of a white woman on the label, drinking in the invitation which it carries. And then comes—opportunity. There follows the hideous episode of the rape and the stake." When readers subsequently charged Irwin with "apologizing for the Negro brute," he firmly denied that such was his intention.[40]

Even in the offices of the *American*, the most sympathetic of the newer journals, crude prejudice provided a counterpoint to the sympathy Baker and other writers revealed in their work. "Darkey," originally a sentimental description of the allegedly carefree rural black, was there applied indiscriminately to all members of the race. "Sounds just like a darkey," an anonymous hand scrawled across the bottom of a letter from Booker Washington's secretary, Emmett Scott. "An Oberlin darkey," another editor commented at the bottom of a request from Ida Hunt Gibbs that "Afro-American" be substituted for "Negro." "Don't mention me to her or she'll blow in for lunch some day." Baker, before he learned better, adopted the jargon naturally. "You would be amused by the darkies here," he wrote his wife when his investigations were underway. "Darkies," and other descriptions of the "savagery" of blacks figured prominently in his earliest installments.[41]

Yet these varying degrees of bias must be set in perspective. If *Pearson's* and *Hampton's*, in a frenetic attempt to revive a wilting genre, exploited racial fears, the ambivalent attitudes in the editorial room of the *American* were probably more typical. Moreover, as important as such bias may have been in muting sympathy or destroying interest, equally significant is the manner in which several muckrakers made their way around it to support the Negro cause. For Sinclair, socialism apparently provided one answer by allowing the translation of "blacks" to "exploited workers." In *The Jungle*, blacks appeared in crude stereotype, a testament to Sinclair's instinctive bias. Yet in the *Appeal to Reason*, the radical weekly to which Sinclair was a frequent contributor, the black worker received a modicum of sympathy because, as was explained, "Socialism regards race problems as secondary to economic problems."[42] Steffens, although his reasoning was less explicit, also supported the Negro cause despite occasional wilingness to indulge popular conceptions concerning the hierarchy of "races." In this hierarchy the "nigger," as he referred to the race in his private letters, clearly ranked lowest. Thus, as Steffens explained to the readers of *Collier's*, the American Negro was inferior to the Japanese on every count, especially when measured by standards of efficiency and organization. Yet such views did not bar Steffens from signing the "Call" for the NAACP, making him one of the two muckrakers to do so.[43]

Charles Edward Russell, like Steffens a signer of the "Call," also believed that race was at root an economic matter. The "Philosophy of Pigment," as he branded racism in his autobiography, was to him reprehensible because it masked class distinction, and denied proper recognition to a fellow professional like W.E.B. DuBois.[44] Baker, sharing many of the biases of his time, and like Russell keenly sensitive to the "tragedy of the mulatto,"[45] also transcended instinctive prejudice to allow a measure of growth. During his early years an idealism inherited from Abolitionist ancestors mingled with the crude bias that infected his home and professional environment. Yet, tutored by Washington, DuBois, and others, he steadily revised both his rhetoric and his outlook between 1905, when his first article on lynching appeared, and 1908 when *Following the Color Line* was complete. Concerned initially with lawlessness more than with the Negro, he provided finally an optimistic vision of racial harmony to be attained through a process of evolution whereby blacks absorbed the values of the white (progressive) middle class.

Editorial policy, a second factor setting limits, made growth difficult, however, and personal prejudice almost irrelevant. "To interest our magazines," wrote William Walling, "a given piece of work must either have very exceptional literary merits, or else must be 'cooked up' in exactly the manner to which the American public is accustomed." Racial bias was no doubt a factor, he conceded, but any subject could be made tempting enough to make editors "overlook their prejudice."[46]

Behind this observation lay an important truth. Progressive reform, insofar as it was spearheaded by various professionals working within the confines of organizations, owed much to the dynamics of these professions. For journalists and editors, certain facts concerning publishing for a mass national audience were crucial. As television and the fate of certain metropolitan dailies illustrate, an audience of millions is no assurance of success if a comparable vehicle for advertising offers relatively greater exposure. With the cost of printing and paper virtually equal to the selling price, as was the case with *McClure's* and the others, advertising was the key to survival. Concern over circulation, dressed up in a seemingly equalitarian devotion to "reader interest," shaped presentation of the Negro issue from first to last.

The appearance of the Schurz article in the January 1904 *McClure's*, often cited as a breakthrough, in fact owed as much to coincidence, even commercial calculation, as to idealism. Contrary to the claim of *McClure's* biographer and others,[47] there is no evidence that the editor solicited the piece, or "contrived a national debate" between the liberal Schurz and Thomas Nelson Page, whose conservative defense of a southern solution followed in successive issues. Rather, both contributions were apparently unsolicited. The Page articles, which McClure judged "a very temperate and interesting expression of the best informed southern opinion."[48] arrived first and might well have appeared alone, thus adding *McClure's* voice to a growing demand to let the south solve the problem. The arrival of the Schurz article coincided with negotiation over the highly prized rights to Schurz's memoirs. If there was an element of concern for the Negro it might have come from Ida Tarbell, who later perfunctorily thanked Schurz for saying "a number of things which need to be said just now."[49]

Whatever the motive, the departure proved temporary. Although the Schurz article, breaking the silence that *McClure's* had maintained on this issue since its founding, boosted circulation to a near-record high, the risks on balance apparently seemed not worth the benefit. The magazine refused a request to open its column to discussion of the Page piece, rejected a second contribution on the subject from Schurz, and in subsequent years turned down material from H.G. Wells, DuBois, and Mary White Ovington. Commenting on the Wells proposal, an editorial assistant voiced the policy of caution. "I felt sure," she wrote to McClure, "you would not for a moment consider this proposition. You know well Mr. Wells' general views and how much antagonism was excited by the work he did for *Harper's* touching upon this difficult problem."[50] After 1905, the Negro appeared in *McClure's* infrequently, most notably in sentimental and patronizing fiction, in another plea from Page to let the South alone, and in a proposal by an English observer that a black state be created, travel rights curtailed, and the Fifteenth Amendment repealed. The Baker articles on lynching, an apparent exception, were as Sam McClure saw it, a case study of the lawlessness of American life, a concern that was an obsession with him at the time of the assignment.[51]

At the *American Magazine* principle was more obviously a factor than at *McClure's*. Baker himself was enthusiastic, quickly shedding the cruder biases that surfaced in his lynching articles. William Allen White, commenting on the proposed series, termed it vital in view of agitation for repeal of the Fifteenth Amendment and several undisclosed "stories Steffens has heard about the Booker Washington school." Editors Bert Boyden, John Siddall, and John Phillips, seeing the favorable publicity the project was engendering, dropped their initial reserve and even appeared on occasion genuinely moved by Baker's findings.[52]

But profit could not be ignored. "Everything depends on the method of treatment," Phillips cautioned the reporter at the outset; "so long as your articles are good journalistically and you can hold the public interest, we can go on with them." At first there seemed to be no problem. "You have been getting us some fine publicity down there in the south," Boyden wrote as Baker launched his study. "It all helps." When Baker strayed,

Phillips gently reminded him of "the importance of working as long as possible with the Southerner of the best type and to the limit." At the same time he urged Baker to revise his second installment. "After all," he lectured, "they are the people whom we wish to reach and enlighten." Baker, to his roots a journalist, and as a partner in the *American* keenly aware that his series could make or break the new venture, never questioned this wisdom. Years later, in his lengthy autobiography, he devoted one paragraph to this work, now widely hailed as his best effort. It was, he remembered, "a 'real success' from the editorial point of view."[53]

Baker's revisions of his articles, revealing the way in which such pressures moderated his instinctive outrage, showed what his concern for "reader interest" meant in practice. Disturbed by evidences of struggle and conflict in American life he tried to reconcile divergent positions, making room for the Washingtons and the DuBoises. On balance, however, the Washington-southern-white-educator group was the greater influence. In his "personal conclusions," for example, Baker accommodated Mary White Ovington, later an organizer of the NAACP, by changing a critical reference to "foolish agitation" to a grudging acknowledgment that "there must always be men like Dr. DuBois." But he also removed, at the request of James Dillard of the Rural Education Board, a lengthy discussion of "social contact." In its place he put a statement that the less said about the issue the better, a direct paraphrase of Dillard's letter on the point. Interestingly it was precisely this sentence that Gunnar Myrdal later cited to illustrate the "static assumption" that governed American thought on the race issue after 1908.[54] In response to Baker, Dillard wrote that he was happy to hear that "the *American* circulation has not lessened in the south," and predicted Baker's book would have a "wide reading." In many respects Baker's accomplishment, the outstanding one of the muckrakers on this issue, testified to the possibilities of personal development. Yet in other ways it was, as Mary White Ovington wrote when his series was complete, "just as much radicalism as . . . a popular magazine will stand."[55]

Financial considerations, indirectly a factor in the general decline of muckraking after 1908,[56] probably also produced reluctance to pursue the race issue further. At any rate, most magazines dropped the issue, making Baker's work the high point of the muckrakers' interest. *Cosmopolitan* and *Collier's* returned to silence on the issue. Although the *American* supported the insurgents in Congress, it too lost interest in the cause of Negro rights long before it became the purveyor of sweet sentimentality for which it was soon noted.[57] *McClure's*, if the NAACP charge concerning the Jane Addams article may be believed, was unwilling to inform its readers of Progressive Party lily-whitism. The discovery by *Hampton's* and *Pearson's* that muckraking could consider the race issue best by pandering to racist sentiment was a frank acknowledgement of the growing mood of reaction, and a significant admission, as Ray Stannard Baker had earlier found out, that the *McClure's* canons had definite limits where race was concerned. Since these same years witnessed a renewed attack on Negro rights, the NAACP, formed in 1909, rightly saw the silence of the press as a major problem and established a press bureau to overcome it. Newspapers, the organization reported on one occasion, could sometimes be pressured. But the magazines remained another matter.[58]

If muted racism and editorial policy limited the interest and tempered the response of the muckrakers, was their influence not salutary nonetheless? The question is a difficult one. Even in the case of Sinclair's *The Jungle*, or Baker's series on the railroads—notable examples of muckrakers' influence in arousing public opinion—cause and alleged effect are imperfectly related. On the race issue such connections are even more tenuous, the evidence more fragmentary. Scattered data suggest that while the muckrakers had little effect on national policy, they stimulated some action on the local level. Moreover, in throwing their weight to the Washington camp in a time of crisis the magazines may well have affected the developing struggle over Negro rights. How one judges this overall impact will clearly depend on an assessment of the local action and the struggle between Washington and his opponents.

National policy remained immune. President Roosevelt's reactions to the *McClure's* articles of Schurz and Baker illustrate the degree to which early muckraking, with no solutions of its own, depended on the energy of public officials in translating indignation into concrete programs. Where irrigation or the railroads were concerned, T.R. was willing. In the case of suffrage restriction and lynching, he was not. Writing Schurz about his "noteworthy article" the President first rehearsed the bold actions he had taken in *other* areas of public concern. "But," he continued, "as regards the race problem in the South I have been greatly puzzled. . . . I feel just as you do about the nullification of the 14th, 15th, and even 13th Amendments in the South; but as it has not as yet seemed absolutely necessary that I should notice this, I have refrained from doing so."[59]

With Baker his dealings were similar. The article on lynching, T.R. wrote Baker, was the best the President had seen anywhere. In private conversation with the reporter he said that the Southerners, in their racial attitudes, were "only overgrown children!"[60] But the public Roosevelt, as recent studies have demonstrated, was rapidly abandoning the Negro.[61] By the time *Following the Color Line* appeared he was openly critical, chastising the reporter for placing too much emphasis on the economic aspects of the race struggle.[62]

Locally the muckrakers' articles had greater impact, although not always that which the modern reader might expect. The movement against peonage (the convict-lease system) which swept the South during the Progressive era may have profited by the exposures in *Cosmopolitan*. Mississippi defeated the system in 1906, and Oklahoma progressives forbade the selling of convict labor the following year, as did Georgia under the administration of Hoke Smith.[63]

Action against lynching and rioting, however, took a less direct form. Praising Baker's study of lynching, a public official in Springfield, Ohio, the scene of one of the ghastlier outrages he described, credited his account with leading to passage of an ordinance prohibiting the use of screens or other obstructions to the view of the interior of saloons after closing hours. This ordinance, Baker wrote in the revision of the article for his book, "has proved of great assistance to the police department in controlling the low saloons where the riot spirit is bred."[64] In Atlanta, as Charles Crowe has shown in tracing the effect of the riots of 1906, reports such as Baker's precipitated a rash of prohibitionist legislation, much of it prejudicial to the interests of lower-class whites and blacks alike.[65] Baker, also reporting this outcome for the book version, again celebrated such reform. In this way Baker's articles, despite his relative sympathy toward the Negro, served an end not unlike the one Will Irwin directly espoused in his article on "Nigger Gin."

More significantly, reports of riots and racial tension stimulated the movement to formalize Jim Crow laws. Again Baker's role is especially revealing. In his reports instinctive outrage over discrimination battled with a desire to dampen struggle by further separating the races. Although he had been told that Jim Crow exacerbated tensions, he finally convinced himself that the uncertainties of the older, informal system were most at fault. Since a formalization of Jim Crow would avoid the "dangers of clashes between the ignorant of both races," such regulations might be allowed as "the inevitable scaffolding of progress." Although he suspected that economic discrimination bred misery, he decided finally that such segregation was producing a vital black business community. Thus, as Allen Spear has remarked, Baker exemplified those of his generation who mistook a forced accommodation to unpleasant realities for something more than it was.[66]

Baker's support of the Washington approach, evidenced in his description of successful black businessmen, was only one instance of the general influence of the press on the developing struggle between Washington and his opponents. The organizers of the NAACP, aware that Baker in particular would be a useful ally, early attempted to interest him in their plan. Although the reporter attended a preliminary organizational meeting, he refused finally to sign the "Call" issued in the late spring of 1909.[67] Subsequently, Baker became increasingly a direct spokesman for the Washington position, in various articles and even in a speech he delivered before the second annual convention of the NAACP.[68] Although the segregation policies of the Wilson administration gave Baker pause, he supported the President in a number of articles, in none of which did he mention the race issue. Although aware of "Gathering Clouds along the Color Line," as he titled an article in 1915, Baker insisted that the race issue demanded "statesmen" not "agitators."[69] In this way, his vision of a harmonious social order, to be achieved if necessary by a "scaffolding" of Jim Crow, reinforced racial attitudes and editorial pressures.

Baker's silence concerning the NAACP, and his continued optimism in the face of racial turmoil, mirrored the position of the popular press in general in the period after 1909. When on one occasion the *Independent* published a piece dealing with the new organization, the enthusiastic reaction of one leader revealed the novelty of the occasion.[70] Although the *Survey* reported annual meetings of the NAACP, and the *Independent* and the *Nation* continued to oppose a deepening pattern of discrimination, the popular magazines were unwilling or unable to mount even the modest indignation of a decade earlier.

For present-day liberal reformers the muckrakers provide both inspiration and a warning. Despite a poisoned ideological atmosphere, professional and institutional restraints, and a deep-seated fear of social disorder, some of these journalists found courage to expose the worst, if not all, of the racial evils of their day. Despite the limitations described here, they broke important ground: in stressing that race was a national issue; in opposing extreme racism of the Thomas Dixon variety; in condemning lynching and extremist demands for further discrimination; perhaps even in furthering a rhetorical revolution whereby readers of the popular magazines learned that the "darkies" of their generation preferred to be called "Negroes," and this name capitalized.

But their shortcomings on the race issue warn how uncertain a vehicle is muckraking in dealing with an issue on which there is little basis in popular feeling for indignation or outraged innocence, no consensus to structure "facts" however scientifically reported. If the Negro had champions during the Progressive era they were most likely to be found in journals with more limited, one might even say highbrow, circulation, journals similar to those which in our own day continue to alert readers to various abuses glossed over by allegedly "liberal" organs of mass opinion. Muckraking, a perennial force in American life, will no doubt continue to inspire reform where there exists a basis for popular indignation. It will be less effective, this survey suggests, where the most powerful forces against change reside not merely in the "interests" but in the "people" themselves.

Notes

1. "The Editor's Plebiscite," *Voice of the Negro*, 4 (1907), 224; "The Muckmakers," ibid., 3 (1906), 401–2; "The Truth," *Crisis*, 5 (1912), 76–77; "Work for Black Folk in 1914," ibid., 7 (1914), 186–87; "The Survey," ibid., 240–41; A.F. Hilger to Baker, June 10, 1916, Ray Stannard Baker Papers, Library of Congress.

2. Louis Filler, *Crusaders for American Liberalism* (New York, 1961), p. 262; H. Wish, "Negro Education and the Progressive Movement," *J. Negro Hist.*, 49 (1964), 184–200; J. Semonche, *Ray Stannard Baker* (Chapel Hill, 1969), pp. 198–210.

3. J.H. Franklin, *From Slavery to Freedom*, 2d ed. (New York, 1956), p. 431; G. Myrdal, *An American Dilemma* (New York, 1944), p. 1022; C. Crowe, "Racial Violence and Social Reform," *J. Negro Hist.*, 53 (1968), 245; H. Shapiro, "The Muckrakers and Negroes," *Phylon*, 31 (1970), 76–88. See also Judson A. Grenier, "The Origins and Nature of Progressive Muckraking" (Ph.D. diss., U.C.L.A., 1965).

4. C.V. Woodward, *The Strange Career of Jim Crow* (New York, 1967); *Origins of the New South* (Baton Rouge, La., 1951), chaps. 12–14; I.A. Newby, *Jim Crow's Defense* (Baton Rouge, La., 1965); H. Blumenthal, "Woodrow Wilson and the Race Question," *J. Negro Hist.*, 48 (1963), 1–21.

5. In the present study "muckrakers" includes writers and editors generally associated with the movement, and any others who contributed articles on race to *McClure's* and other magazines generally associated with the "new journalism." Specifically, attention has been paid to the public writings (and private papers where available) of the individuals Judson Grenier, in "Progressive Muckraking," pp. 35–36, includes among first-, second-, and third-rank contributors: (1)*Steffens, *Tarbell, *Baker, *Russell, *Lawson, *Phillips (David Graham), McClure, *Adams,

*Sinclair, Sullivan; (2)*Lewis, *Irwin, Hampton, N. Hapgood, *Hendrick, Connolly, J.S. Phillips, Flower, Flynt, *Turner; (3) Creel, Spargo, Mathews, Welliver, Dorr, Hard, Myers, Boyden. Those indicated by asterisks contributed forty percent of the 2000 articles in the muckraking genre that appeared between 1903 and 1912, according to D. Chalmers, "The Muckrakers and the Growth of Corporate Power," *Am. J. Econ. and Soc.*, 18 (1959), 295–311.

6. E. Cassady, "Muckraking in the Gilded Age," *Am. Lit.*, 13 (1941), 134–41; J.C. Clark, "Reform Currents in the Polite Monthly Magazines, 1880–1900," *Mid-America*, 47 (1965), 3–23.

7. For background see Warren F. Kuhl, *Hamilton Holt* (Gainesville, Fla., 1960), chaps. 2–4. Comparison of magazines is based on articles appearing under "Negro" and related headings in the *Reader's Guide*, and on sampling of the files of the various periodicals.

8. W.E. Walling, "Race War in the North," *The Independent*, 65 (1908), 529–35; C.F. Kellogg, *The NAACP, 1909–20* (Baltimore, 1967), p. 10.

9. "The 'Decline' of Lynching," *Crisis*, 8 (1914), 19. On Abbott see Ira Brown, *Lyman Abbott* (Cambridge, Mass., 1953).

10. A. Grimes, *The Political Liberalism of the New York Nation* (Chapel Hill, 1953), pp. 5–12, 68, 121.

11. For a brief mention of Flower and the Negro see H. Cline, "Flower and the *Arena*," *Journalism Quart.*, 17 (1940), 255. The statement is based on analysis of the *Arena* from 1890 to 1900.

12. *Charities*, 15 (1905).

13. Rayford Logan, *The Negro in American Life and Thought* (New York, 1954), pp. 239–74. This judgment is echoed in Shapiro, "The Muckrakers and Negroes," p. 77.

14. W.E.B. DuBois, ed., "The College Bred Negro," *Atlanta University Publications, Report of the Fifth Conference* (Atlanta, Ga., 1900), p. 9.

15. "Reconstruction and Disfranchisement," *Atlantic Monthly*, 88 (1901), 435–36; A. Sledd, "The Negro: Another View," ibid., 90 (1902), 65–73; C.F. Smith, "Sledd and Emory College," *Nation*, 75 (1902), 245. See also Bliss Perry to B. Washington, Aug. 16, 1902, Washington Papers, Library of Congress.

16. R.W. Gilder to C. Schurz, July 8, 22, 30, 1903, Carl Schurz Papers, Library of Congress; for other *Century* articles see C.F. Adams, "Reflex Light from Africa," 72 (1906), 101–11, and R.B. Bean, "The Negro Brain," ibid., 778–84.

17. *McClure's*, *Everybody's*, *Cosmopolitan*, and other representatives of the "New Journalism" gained circulations of 400,000 and above, whereas the most popular of the older monthlies totaled about 100,000 or less.

18. C. Schurz, "Can the South Solve the Negro Problem," *McClure's*, 22 (1904), 259–75. To a friend Schurz wrote: "I have touched the moral and ideal aspect of the matter but slightly and confined myself more to practical considerations, wishing to produce a certain practical effect upon the better class of Southerners without distinction of party." Schurz to M. Storey, Aug. 5, 1903, Carl Schurz Papers.

19. J.S. Phillips to Schurz, Jan. 4, 28, 1904, Carl Schurz Papers.

20. Booker T. Washington to Schurz, Dec. 28, 1903; Hugh M. Browne to C. Schurz, Jan. 18, Feb. 19, 25, May 12, 1904; Ethel O. Mason to Schurz, Apr. 28, 1904; P.E. Hopkins to Schurz, Mar. 15, 1904; H.T. Kalling to Schurz, Mar. 16, 1904, Mary C. Terrell to *McClure's*, Jan. 29, 1904, Carl Schurz Papers.

21. Baker, "What Is Lynching?" *McClure's*, 24 (1905), 299–314, 422–30; Ward, "Peonage in America," *Cosmopolitan*, 39 (1905), 423–30.

22. Gladden, "The Negro Crisis," *American*, 63 (1907), 296–301; Baker's series

appeared monthly, March to August 1907, and February to September 1908.

23. *American*: B.F. Young, "Big Frank," 64, 361–71; L. Finch, "The Slaves Who Stayed," 64, 551–53, 65, 132–35, 67, 395–97; M. Herzberg, "The Negro's Dogs," 65, 160; H. Rion, "The Marragemony of Minerva White," 67, 24–28; H. Kemp, "On Hearing Negro Girls' Songs," 67, 427; R. Jonas, "Jim Crow Car," 67, 553.

24. Barry, "Slavery in the South Today," *Cosmopolitan*, 42 (1907), 481–91. An additional evidence of interest in 1907 was J.S. Williams, "Negro and the South," *Metropolitan*, 27 (1907), 137–51.

25. N. Hapgood to Baker, Nov. 16, 1906, Apr. 18, 1907, Baker Papers, Library of Congress; "Meaning of Peonage," *Collier's*, 43 (1909), 26; W.E. Chancellor, "Washington's Race Question," ibid., 42 (Oct. 3, 1908), 24–25; cf. T. Dixon, "The Debt of the Law to the Lawless," ibid., 36 (1905), 21–22, and comment, 9.

26. T.N. Page, "The Great American Question," *McClure's*, 28 (1907), 565–72; R. Jonas, "Sermon in Black and White," ibid., 30 (1908), 360; H.M. Kelly "Heritage of Ham," ibid., 31 (1908), 277–90; E.E. Peake, "Jungle Blood," ibid., 510–21; W. Archer, "Black and White in the South," ibid., 33 (1909), 324–38.

27. For a general discussion of this change see David M. Chalmers, *The Social and Political Ideas of the Muckrakers* (New York, 1964), and his "The Muckrakers and the Growth of Corporate Power"; on Baker see R. Bannister, *Ray Stannard Baker* (New Haven, 1966), and J. Semonche, *Ray Stannard Baker* (Chapel Hill, 1969).

28. For initial plan see Editorial Note, *American*, 63 (1907), 301; Baker, "What to Do about the Negro," ibid., 66 (1908), 463–70.

29. In 1904 Russell made a personal contribution of $1000 to establish a scholarship at Fisk University. See E.C. Stickel to Russell, May 14, 1904. Kellogg, *NAACP*, pp. 298–99.

30. Dickson, "The Unknowable Negro," *Hampton's*, 22 (1909), 729–42; "The Negro in Politics," ibid., 23 (1909), 225–36; "Exit the Black Man," ibid., 497–505; R. Wooley, "The South's Fight for Race Purity," *Pearson's*, 23 (1910), 3–11; B.D. Rivera, "Great Black Plague," ibid., 417–20; A. Hale, "Why Miscegenation Flourishes in the North," ibid., 543–51; M. Hayson, "The Negro as a Poet," *Twentieth Century*, 1 (1910), 332–38; [editorial], "Is Caucasian Cowardice Congenital?," ibid. 5 (1912), 8–9.

31. This statement is based on examination of the autobiographies of Norman Hapgood, Will Irwin, S.S. McClure, Upton Sinclair, Lincoln Steffens, Ida Tarbell, and William Allen White.

32. Frederick S. Monroe to Schurz, Jan. 22, 1904, Carl Schurz Papers.

33. I.A. Newby, *Jim Crow's Defense* (La. State Univ. Press, 1965); C.V. Woodward, *Origins of the New South* (La. State Univ. Press, 1951), chaps. 12–14; H. Shapiro, "The Muckrakers and Negroes."

34. Grenier, "Progressive Muckraking," p. 61.

35. White to Hazel McDaniel, Oct. 22, 1912, *Selected Letters of William Allen White*, ed. Walter Johnson (New York, 1947), pp. 137–38; see also White to Walter Thueing, Dec. 12, 1906, William Allen White Papers, Library of Congress; White, *The Autobiography of William Allen White* (New York, 1946), pp. 630–34.

36. Tarbell to C. Schurz, Sept. 28, 1903, Carl Schurz Papers.

37. Riis, "The Black Half," *Crisis*, 5 (1913), 298–99. See also Riis to R. Baker, Apr. 2, 1907 on his "exasperation" at the southerner's position, Baker Papers, Library of Congress.

38. See note 30. The quotation is from an editorial note in *Pearson's*, 23 (1910), 543.

39. "Editorial Note," *Hampton's*, 23 (1909), 225; editorial note, *Pearson's*, 23 (1910), 3.

40. Irwin, "The American Saloon," *Collier's*, 41 (1908), 9–10; "More About 'Nigger Gin'," ibid. (1908), 27–30.

41. Handwritten comments on E. Scott to Baker, Apr. 7, 1908, and Ida G. Hunt to Baker, May 30, 1908, Baker Papers, Library of Congress; Baker to Jessie Baker, Mar. 15, 1906, Baker Papers in possession of James S. Baker; Baker, "Clashes of Races in a Southern City," *American*, 44 (1907), 15, 18; cf. *Following the Color Line*, pp. 39, 44.

42. Sinclair, *The Jungle*, quoted in Shapiro, "Muckrakers," 80; "Negroes and the Race Problem," *Appeal*, Mar. 28, 1908.

43. Steffens's "Race War in Harlem," New York *Evening Post*, July 18, 1896, described the conflict between Italians and other whites in the northern Manhattan community. Harry Stein writes: "Steffens commonly used the term "nigger" which his editors, Hicks and Winter, always changed to 'Negro' in the two-volume published letters." July 25, 1969, personal communication; Steffens, "California and the Japanese," *Collier's*, 57 (1916), 5, 36.

44. Russell, speech at Quinn Chapel, Chicago, Illinois, Nov. 29, 1912, MS. Charles E. Russell Papers, Library of Congress; *Leaving It to the South* (New York, 1912); *Bare Hands and Stone Walls* (New York, 1933), pp. 219–25.

45. Baker, "Tragedy of the Mulatto," *American*, 65 (1908), 582–98. Baker's special concern for the mulatto, and his instinctive feeling that white "blood" produced accomplishment and greater sensitivity to suffering drew criticism from many readers on the left. See for example Mary W. Ovington to Baker, Apr. 13, 1907, and "A friend" to Baker, Apr. 24, 1908, Baker Papers.

46. Walling to Mary C. Terrell, Apr. 7, 1910, Mary Church Terrell Papers, Library of Congress.

47. Peter Lyon, *Success Story* (Deland, Fla., 1967), p. 253; Filler, *Crusaders*, p. 258; Shapiro, "Muckrakers," 81.

48. McClure to Schurz, Sept. 22, 1903, Schurz Papers.

49. J. Phillips to Schurz, Jan. 25, 1904, Aug. 31, Sept. 3, 1903; I. Tarbell to Schurz, Sept. 28, 1903, Schurz Papers.

50. J.S. Phillips to C. Schurz, Jan. 25, June 3, 1904, Schurz Papers; Mary L. Bisland to S.S. McClure, Dec. 19, 1907, S.S. McClure Papers, Indiana University; Francis L. Broderick, *W.E.B. DuBois* (Stanford, 1959), p. 59; M. Ovington, *Crisis*, 32 (1926), cited in Kellogg, *NAACP*, p. 6.

51. Peake, "Jungle Blood"; Page, "Great American Question"; Archer, "Black and White"; McClure, "S.S. Remarks to Staff," ca. Oct. 1, 1904, wrote "A man's life is less safe from violence in the United States than in any country of Europe excepting Russia," McClure Papers. See also McClure, "Increase of Lawlessness in the United States," *McClure's*, 24 (1904), 163–71.

52. White to J.S. Phillips, Oct. 22, 1906, Baker Papers; A.A. Boyden to Baker (1907?); J.M. Siddall to Baker, Dec. 28, 1907; J.S. Phillips to Baker, Jan. 25, May 22, 1907, Baker Papers, Library of Congress.

53. Baker, "Draft for American Chronicle," MS. Baker Papers, 433; A.A. Boyden to Baker, Nov. 27, 1906; J.S. Phillips to Baker, Apr. 18, 1907, Baker Papers, Library of Congress; Baker, *American Chronicle* (New York, 1945), p. 238. Ida Tarbell, also thinking first of the magazine, wrote Baker Aug. 9, 1907: "Your work has been a wonderful thing for us all this year," Baker Papers. J.M. Siddall to Baker, Dec. 28, 1907, summarized circulation statistics and concluded: "This, according to the wise guys, is a pretty good showing," Baker Papers, Library of Congress.

54. M. Ovington to Baker, Aug. 19, 21, 1908, Baker Papers, Library of Congress. For the change compare Baker, "What to Do About the Negro," 468, and *Following the Color Line*, p. 304, ll. 23–28. For his accommodation to Dillard, see James Dillard to Baker, June 24, 1908, Baker Papers, Library of Congress, and *Following the Color Line*, p. 305, ll. 10–16.

55. J. Dillard to Baker, July 6, 1908; M. Ovington to Baker, Aug. 21, 1908, Baker Papers, Library of Congress.

56. This is not to say that the advertisers simply "muzzled" the press; however, the financial climate following the panic of 1907 led to increased concern with circulation. For a discussion of the literature on this subject see C.C. Regier, *The Era of the Muckrakers* (Chapel Hill, 1932); and for the difficulties of one magazine, J. Semonche, "The *American Magazine* . . . ," *Journalism Quart.*, 40 (1963), 36–44, 86.

57. Semonche, "The *American Magazine*," pp. 36–44, 86.

58. NAACP, "Report of 5th session," May 5, 1914; M. Nerney (secretary to NAACP) to Florence Kelly, Sept. 18, 1913, wrote: "The problem of publicity is awful. Every magazine, practically, in New York is closed to us. It is my firm belief that there is not a magazine or newspaper in New York City without its Bourbon." Both in NAACP Papers, Library of Congress.

59. Roosevelt to C. Schurz, Dec. 24, 1903, *The Letters of Theodore Roosevelt*, edited by E. Morison (8 vols., Cambridge, Mass., 1951–54), III, pp. 679–82.

60. Roosevelt to Baker, Jan. 2, 1905, quoted in Baker, *American Chronicle*, 192; Baker, Journal C (Jan. 28, 1905), 58, MS. in Baker Papers, Library of Congress; Seth Scheiner, "President Roosevelt and the Negro, 1900–1908," *J. Negro Hist.*, 47 (1962), 169–82.

61. Seth Scheiner, "President Roosevelt and the Negro," *J. Negro Hist.*, 47 (1962), 169–82.

62. Roosevelt to Baker, June 3, 1908, *Letters*, VI, p. 1046.

63. Woodward, *Origins of the New South*, p. 424.

64. Stewart L. Tatum to Baker, Mar. 5, 1905, Baker Papers, Library of Congress; Baker, *Following the Color Line*, p. 210.

65. Crowe, "Racial Violence"; Baker, *Following the Color Line*, p. 25.

66. Baker, *Following the Color Line*, p. 305; A. Spear, *Black Chicago* (Chicago, 1967), 7.

67. W. Walling to Baker, Feb. 6, Mar. 5, 22, 1909, Baker Papers, Library of Congress. Although Kellogg, *NAACP*, pp. 297–301, cites Baker as having signed the copy of the "Call" in the Villard Papers, he apparently removed his name before the final copy of the list was circulated. See Warren D. St. James, *The NAACP* (New York, 1958), p. 40.

68. Baker, "Negro in a Democracy," *The Independent*, 67 (Sept. 9, 1909), 584–88; Baker to B.T. Washington, Apr. 29, 1910, mentioned in Washington to Baker, May 3, 1910, Baker Papers, Library of Congress; Baker, "Negro Suffrage in a Democracy," *Atlantic Monthly*, 106 (1910), 612–19.

69. Baker, "Gathering Clouds," *World's Work*, 32 (1916), 232–36; "Statesman of the Negro Problem," ibid., 35 (1918), 306–11.

70. [NAACP secretary] to Joel E. Springarn, Oct. 15, 1912, NAACP Papers.

Law, Justice, and the Muckrakers

David M. Chalmers

In the late 1960s "Law and Order" became a battle cry. Combined with another emotion-laden phrase, "Crime in the Streets," it did much to elect a president of the United States. In the competitive sloganeering which marks great political contests, attempted substitutes such as "Law and Justice" and "Justice and Order" did not seem to make their point. Soaring crime rates, the insecurity of big-city streets, ghetto riots, political riots, Vietnam riots, police riots, youth riots, school riots, long hair, dirty pictures, and the drug scene seemed combined to offer proof of societal malfunction.

In 1965, "recognizing the urgency of the nation's crime problem," President Lyndon Johnson had set up a commission to look into it all. When the "Crime Commission" reported in 1967, it avoided calling for redefinition of crime, institutional replacement, or social reconstruction, but it stated that in 1965, more than two million Americans went to prison or juvenile training school, or were placed on probation. About forty per cent of all male children now living in the United States, it estimated, would be arrested at some time in their lives for a nontraffic offense. "In sum," the Commission said, "America's system of criminal justice is overcrowded, undermanned, underfinanced, and very often misunderstood."[1] Successive national Riot and Violence Commission reports have been less restrained in their discussion of the shortcomings of law and justice in America, and a growing number of young (and sometimes older) militants, black and white, have felt no need to show any restraint at all.

All of this has been chronicled in the press and the media, which have not infrequently been accused of living on, catering to, and accelerating— if, indeed, they did not on occasion stage—the unrest. How are the justice-delivery systems doing in America? Read the quarterly *Uniform Crime Reports* of the F.B.I., or the news columns of your local paper. Try to find something on the radio and TV state and local-news programs other than crime, violence, and city-commission meetings. Try walking along city streets late at night without looking back over your shoulder. Read Jeanne Dixon's prophecies. Turn to the *New York Times* for reports on police protection of gamblers or where judges get their campaign funds. Reflect on the Chicago conspiracy trial, where the government and the judge did their best to put away the nation's dissent leaders for a newly made-up crime that had probably not been committed. Read the words of the president of Yale University against holding a trial for a murder which someone must have committed. Observe crowd provocation to police and police assault on crowds. Read the American Jewish Committee's report on sentencing in Southern courts, or the Civil Rights Commission report on justice for the Mexican-Americans in the Southwest, or watch what happens when policemen are tried for brutality or ghetto murder. Meditate on Howard James's eleven categories of judicial incompetence, in his 1968 Pulitzer Prize-winning "Crisis in the Courts" for *The Christian Science Monitor*.[2]

In its search for the causes, the national Crime Commission explained that the transformation of America from a relatively relaxed rural society into a tumultuous urban one had overtaxed the traditional methods of the criminal-justice system, commenting on the great inertia of that system, whose lower courts had been deemed scandalous by the Wickersham Commission more than thirty years before.[3]

The Riot Commission report, in 1968, added another dimension. Behind the functional problems of law and justice in an urbanized American society were some three hundred years of injustice to the black, which the Commission catchily described as "white racism." When the assassination of Robert Kennedy (and perhaps that of Martin Luther King) led the president to set up yet another commission—this one on the causes and prevention of violence—one of two things seemed clear: Either (1) the distribution of rewards, opportunities, and justice in America had changed somewhere along the way, and *that* was the problem, or (2) the American system of distributing rewards, opportunities, and justice had *not* changed along the way and *that* was the problem. The Violence Commission reports offered another dimension, pointing out that (1) violence and civil strife have been a continuous part of the American pattern, and (2) the society's justice-delivery system had never been prepared to deal with it.

Anyone who has read commission task-force reports, taken part in court-watcher programs, been involved with the treatment of the poor, the black, the hippie, the dissenter, or the radical, or covered their treatment for the media has seen another part of the law-and-justice system. Beneath human error and crudity, the justice system in any society is enmeshed in the arrangements of the existing order—that is, the existing distribution of rewards, opportunity, and treatment. Justice, in almost all societies, has a strictly within-the-system meaning. The definitions of crime are taken as given and eternal, and order means the security of life and existing social arrangements from violent threat or disruption. Law is the admittedly imperfect though presumably impartial instrument. Violence is the monopoly of legal authority, and criminal in the hands of others. If justice really consists in giving every man his due, the existing order does much to define what that due is.

Where did it all begin? Like the anxious parent, let us ask the question: "What did we do wrong?"

By the beginning of this century, the Americans had built their national industrial system. The foreign and domestic immigrant tides were flowing into cities, and the municipal transportation systems were exploding the cities out toward the suburbs. A group of able, hardworking journalists stumbled into offering a comprehensive national survey and stock-taking to an enlarged magazine-reading, middle-class public. What was the state of law and justice and what did the journalists of exposure have to say about it? Specifically, how did these journalists perceive the functioning of the justice-delivery system? What did the muckrakers think was going on in the streets, the police stations, the courts, and the prisons?

Life sixty-five years ago was pretty rough. The experts weren't very happy about the quality of criminal statistics, but there was general agreement that conditions were bad, crime high, cities ungovernable. According to the universally quoted Chicago *Tribune* compilations, the murder rate had leveled off at almost nine thousand yearly, up some seven hundred percent in less than a quarter of a century. Today, with more than two and a half times the population, our yearly total is only a third more. On the base currently used by the F.B.I.'s Crime Reports, the Progressive era homicide rate ran about eleven per one hundred thousand, as compared to less than eight today. According to the 1970 statistics, the national murder capitals were Charlotte, North Carolina; Augusta and Atlanta,

Georgia; and Greenville, South Carolina; at between twenty and twenty-five per hundred thousand. During the muckrake era, Murdertown, U.S.A., was Memphis, Tennessee, which could yearly be counted upon for forty to ninety per hundred thousand, more than twice the rate of its nearest competitor, Atlanta. New York could only produce five murders per hundred thousand, and Chicago, seven. There had been 131,951 homicides in the United States over the preceding two decades, William Howard Taft told a Yale Law School audience in a much-reported address in 1906, "As murder is on the increase," he continued, "so are all offenses of the felony class."[4]

The previous year, James Elbert Cutler had begun his comprehensive study of a uniquely American form of violence with the statement: "It has been said that our country's national crime is lynching." Although the yearly average had leveled off below a hundred, less than half the annual carnage of the preceding decades, it was still a matter of widely expressed concern. But homicide and lynching were retail violence and the 1906 rioters of Atlanta proceeded to do it wholesale, killing more than twenty-five blacks and otherwise visiting mayhem as widely as possible, an example followed in Abraham Lincoln's Springfield, two years later. Industrial violence was reaching what was to be its highest level in American history. Although the automobile was not yet adding its killer contribution to the statistics, forcible rape was beginning its recorded rise, for which a later explanation inclined to divide credit between Mr. Ford's wonderful contribution to American sex education, and the greater propensity of middle-class girls to protest about it afterwards.[5]

To contemporary professional observers, a long-building crisis was emerging within the national justice-delivery system. In 1908, President Taft stated that:

> If one were to be asked in what respect we have fallen farthest short of the ideal conditions in our whole Government, I think he would be justified in answering, in spite of the glaring defects in our system of municipal government, that it is our failure to secure expedition and thoroughness in the enforcement of public and private rights in our courts.[6]

Procedure was too elaborate, delays too long, costs too high—particularly for the poor—juries too lenient, appeals too frequent, and reversals too easily and unwarrantedly granted on nonsubstantial technicalities. Taft had already begun to speak out on the failure of the administration of criminal justice before a young Nebraska lawyer named Roscoe Pound offered a much-quoted address to the American Bar Association in 1906 on "The Causes of Popular Dissatisfaction with the Administration of Justice." Agitation was growing within the profession for reform of practice in both civil and criminal cases. In 1907, the ABA set up a special committee "To Suggest Remedies and Formulate Proposed Laws to Prevent Delay and Unnecessary Cost in Litigation," and the *Journal* of the newly formed American Institute of Criminal Law and Criminology poured forth article after note after editorial on the seriousness of the problem.[7]

This rising concern can be summed up in some twelve points:

1. There had been a major increase in the number of crimes, particularly violent ones.

2. This had been made more serious by a breakdown in what was called "the administration of justice." The undue complexity and costliness of the law denied justice to the poor and protected the rich.

3. The slowness and rigidity of the American system compared very unfavorably with efficient British justice.

4. Particularly in the case of homicide, swifter and more certain justice, leading to an increase in the number of convictions and executions, was necessary to serve as a proper deterrent.

5. Overt corruption, particularly at the municipal level, was widespread. The law was subverted by the boss rule.

6. Under this system, the police were partial toward employers, property, and the wealthy, protected crime and vice, and used violence against working people and the poor.

7. Among all the legal reform movements, none was as widely praised as the juvenile courts, pioneered in Rhode Island and Chicago, and best known in the hands of Judge Ben Lindsey in Denver, Colorado.

8. Despite various reform efforts, the same public interest had not been focused on punishment and correction, although the chain gang and the convict-lease system excited the greatest concern.

9. Although union violence caused alarm, judicial prejudices and purchase set the law on the side of capital, overlooking and often supporting various force tactics against labor.

10. The Negro and the urban immigrant were singled out as major contributors to crime and violence, a role which was variously attributed to social environment and to inherent criminality.

11. The alarming prevalence of lynching was particularly blamed on a

popular lack of faith in a malfunctioning criminal-justice system.

12. Because of its many inefficiencies, partialities, and failures, a wide-spread disrespect for the law existed in America.

Such, then was the informed outlook of the times. Where did the journalists of exposure fit in? What did they have to contribute? In the January 1903 number of his magazine, S.S. McClure published his famous editorial, "Concerning Three Articles in This Number of McClure's and a Coincidence That May Set Us Thinking":

> Capitalists, workingmen, politicians, citizens—all breaking the law, or letting it be broken. Who is left to uphold it? The lawyer? Some of the best lawyers in this country are hired, not to go into court to defend cases, but to advise corporations and business firms how they can get around the law without too great a risk of punishment. The judges? Too many of them so respect the laws that for some "error" or quibble they restore to office and liberty men convicted on evidence overwhelmingly convincing to common sense. The churches? We know of one, an ancient and wealthy establishment, which had to be compelled by a Tammany hold-over health officer to put its tenements in sanitary condition. The colleges? They do not understand.[8]

The way the muckrakers saw their central problem was as conflict between the explosive growth of large-scale private economic power (variously called "the Trusts," "the System," "the Interests," "High" or "Frenzied Finance," "Business," "the corporations," or "Accumulated Wealth") and a value and institutional system which could not handle it. The result was known as "corruption" or "lawlessness." The problem of "law and justice" for the Progressive era was one of protection in both the streets and the market place. The widely used term "lawlessness" described both interchangeably. The result was a fair degree of confusion over whether felonious assault, institutional malfunction, or the "aggressions of capital" were being discussed.[9]

The question they faced—or avoided facing—is not an easily resolved one, particularly in times of rapid change: To what degree are the criminal codes which govern the behavior of individuals capable of governing the economic strategies of large organizations? There was an inclination among the muckrakers to assume that they should do so, and that the opening of an unwarranted gap lay at the bottom of the national "lawlessness." Ray Stannard Baker criticized the use of the corporate form as a means by which "reputable people" could "participate in the profits of disreputable business enterprises without disturbing their moral complacency," and Will Irwin argued that the basic purpose of the muckrake crusade was to educate the people to the realization that "the crime of stealing the means of production through corrupt legislatures and corrupt market manipulations" was as serious as "the crime of stealing silver spoons from the safe of a wealthy burgher." [10] The failure to perceive the identity and, perhaps, the failure of society to provide the proper legislative rules so that the identity could be maintained, lay at the core of muckraker perception of the problem. It would be difficult to say that we have yet arrived, in our own day, at any way out of this quandary.

On the general topic of crime in the streets, the muckrakers had little to say. S.S. McClure gave it a go in an editorial on "The Increase of Lawlessness in the United States," based on the Chicago *Tribune* homicide statistics. Commenting on the more favorable European record, he sought to connect the high level of American violence with the widespread corruption his writers had been describing. Could blackmailing and crime-protecting policemen, aldermanic looters, and the ruling combinations of vice-lords, franchise-grabbing capitalists, cooperating politicians, and businessmen-bribers and their lawyers produce a safe society? [11] If this was meant as a rallying cry and research direction, McClure's writers did not respond. Nor did they follow the popular propensity to find a solution in either the British legal system or increased capital punishment.

From the viewpoint of concerned lawyers and judges, the great faults and the problem facing justice were procedural. To a majority of the muckrakers, they were substantive and substantial. The courts played an inconspicuous role in Lincoln Steffens's political exposes and Ida Tarbell's Standard Oil history, but most of the muckrakers found the story relatively simple and pretty bad. The courts "serve business," Samuel Hopkins Adams reported. They were "controlled," according to David Graham Phillips; part of the "trust" system, according to Upton Sinclair and Charles Edward Russell; and of the "class system," by training, association, environment, and interest, Gustavus Myers wrote in his muckraker-socialist *History of the Supreme Court* in 1912. [12]

Though a number of the journalists had covered the police-court beat during their beginning newspaper days, they had not penetrated far enough into the court system to be much concerned about its workings. Generally, it took a specific experience or interest to get them involved even a little. Samuel Hopkins Adams watched the courts whittle down the pure food laws and got mad: "To bend the law itself in the coils of legal procedure, to subvert the people's expressed will by the strategy and chicanery of court or commission," he railed, "was more dangerous than the 'anarchy' of dynamite or of 'the crimson flag.' "[13] Ray Stannard Baker, rubbing his bruises after losing the one libel suit that went against the muckrakers, believed that he had lost because of legal confusion and technicalities. In his notebooks he damned the judges as defenders of the railroad corporations and trusts, holding back "every sort of economic and social change by strict interpretations of ancient law."[14] The journalists continued to complain that regulatory legislation was being gutted by a probusiness judiciary, that the corporations stood above the law, and that the competitor or wronged citizen was kept from his rights by the law's costliness and delays.

Only two of the magazine writers, however, were either inclined or prepared to venture very far into the operation of the courts themselves. Christopher Powell Connolly was a lawyer and one-time prosecuting attorney of Butte, Montana. He had built his reputation among the muckrakers through covering celebrated labor trials and in helping prepare *Collier's* case against the Alaskan land policies of the Taft Administration, during the sensational Pinchot-Ballinger controversy. Carl Snyder, a journalist later to turn economist and head the statistical section of the New York Federal Reserve Bank and the American Statistical Association, seems to have missed belonging to the inner comradeships and public recognition of muckraking. Nevertheless, in addition to serving as an explicator of scientific discovery, he had written a guide to railroad stocks and muckraked several of the railroad magnates. During the winter of 1911–1912, in *Collier's*, he wrote the longest and most forceful series to appear in the magazines about the breakdown of the American judicial system.

Snyder's articles began without fanfare and with no intial series title, although editorial footnotes soon advanced from referring to it as "Scandals of the Law" to "The Scandal of the Lawless Law." While there was no formal connection between Connolly's and Snyder's exposes, *Collier's* ran a note at the bottom of one of Snyder's installments announcing Connolly's forthcoming efforts in *Everybody's*:

> Drastic as is Mr. Snyder's exposure of "The Scandal of the Lawless Law," he covers only a phase of the subject. For eighteen months past C.P. Connolly, on behalf of "Everybody's Magazine," has been investigating the relations between the Judiciary and the Interests, and his series, "The Beast on the Bench," revealing almost incredible conditions, will begin in the February issue of that publication.[15]

When Connolly's articles began to appear, they did so under the less naturalistic title of "Big Business and the Bench." This was not his first effort at muckraking the courts. He had already written on the buying of the law by the feuding copper kings of Montana, how its loopholes had let labor dynamiters escape in Idaho, and of its abuse by "Interest" judges in Colorado. The central problem, he now explained, stemmed from the subservience, conservativeness and property-orientation of the bench, combined with procedural rigidity, red tape, and blind worship of form. As a solution, he called for simplification of procedure, swifter action, shorter decisions, the recall of judicial decisions, and less conservative judges. In his opposition to judicial review, he rejected the philosophy of judicial activism which both he and Snyder saw as an instrument of economic conservatism. As the one lawyer in the muckrake pack, Connolly had little deep or new to say about the justice profession and systems, and even less about how his desired reforms might be brought about. Rather he followed already familiar paths, although perhaps tying in more closely the "administration of justice" complaints of the bar with the antibusiness-privilege howls of the pack.[16]

It was the nonlawyer Carl Snyder who offered the fullest view of the justice crisis.[17] He too protested the economic conservatism of the bench, but, as though operating along some unspoken division of tasks, he left this topic to Connolly. Like S.S. McClure in his 1904 editorial, Snyder focused on the prevalence of murder in America—the worst record of civilized nations—and the huge, clumsy, politics-ridden machinery that permitted eighty-six out of eighty-seven perpetrators to escape the gallows. While he graphically quantified the national homicidal frenzy, Snyder's perception of causes and solutions was less clear. He carefully absolved the immigrant. "Our foreign-born population," he wrote and illustrated, "is far more orderly and less murderous than the native-born." The second generation, under the American influence, and the young were most at fault. Nevertheless, the immigrant along with the Negro suffered because of discrimination and because of the absence of money and influence to produce the miscarriages of justice necessary to gain freedom. Too often, others escaped punishment because of antiquated legal procedure, corrupt governors, and an "imbecile mania of reversing and upsetting decisions."

The solution for judicial malfunction, he once opined, was to take the whole system away from the legal profession. "I believe that there can be no reform worth the powder," he wrote, "until the whole question of crime and punishment is taken from the hands of prosecuting attorneys, of defending lawyers, of juries, judges, and courts of appeal, and put into the hands of men trained to utterly different ethics and ideas—that is, sociologists, criminologists, and physicians." [18] His view of who actually committed crime was less unorthodox, for he fluctuated vaguely between blaming it on professional criminals, inadequate social organization, and "mental, moral, and physical defectives."

But for Snyder the real problem was not so much crime as it was "The Monstrous Breakdown of Criminal Law" which had made the administration of justice into "a Scandal and a Farce." The fault was that of the legal profession and, most of all, the judges. The administration of the law was an anarchy. Neither citizen, lawyer, nor judge could say what the law was. "Justice" was the last man's guess. The judges, like Chinese Mandarins, trifled with the law at whim, writing their conservative ideas into it, hampering it with delay and ruinously high costs of litigation, and overruling decisions at pleasure on grounds not touching the merits of the cases. Although law school deans, judges, governors, and the president of the United States protested, they did so in vain. While England had reformed her system and gained "the leadership of the world in swift and accurate justice," the American crisis only deepened. As Carl Snyder reported it, the bar and the bench remained the greatest obstacle to justice in America.

The Connolly series seemed to stir up relatively little popular interest, and the Snyder articles even less. Perhaps by 1911 the muckrake bolt had been shot. Perhaps it was the issue itself. The "administration of justice" crises just do not seem deeply to touch middle-class imagination and concern. Justice reform has historically been a professional's cause, remote from popular crusades. Repeated revelations about the conditions of policing, the courts, the jails, and the prisons, have not changed the popular disinclination basically to alter the pattern, or sufficiently to fund the national justice-delivery system.

The magazine-reading public found much more drama in the battles of the reformers against the bosses. The muckrakers wrote a good deal about urban corruption, but there was surprisingly little systematic analysis of the relationships between the magistrates, the police, crime, vice, and politics. Usually the journalists got the heart of their stories from local reformers. Sometimes they did impressive digging. The muckrakers publicized the tie-ups between gambling, prostitution, theft, the saloon, the local political machine, the police, and the lower criminal courts. Most of them tended to anchor it in the American business system. G.K. Turner testified before grand juries investigating prostitution. Lincoln Steffens particularly tried to help the election of reform administrations. The magazine journalists greatly heightened popular awareness of corruption, but it seems not too harsh to say that conditions were not much different and the understanding not much deepened when they got done.[19]

Nor did the muckrakers have much specific impact on the parole, probation, and juvenile court movements. The "kids' courts" were a favorite topic of the magazine press, but the muckrakers passed over it almost completely. William Hard and Upton Sinclair had something to say about child labor, and Lincoln Steffens wrote at length about the "Just Judge" Ben Lindsey[20] (who himself came to write for the magazines), but this crusade was not theirs.

Similarly, prison reform and penal brutality did not substantially engage the muckrakers' energies. Single stories about peonage on southern railroad construction and the slave-labor contracts of the lease system in the South were one-shot affairs. Charles Edward Russell's 1909 series on the use of beatings, water cures, and torture by electricity (none of them unknown to more recent American penology) was a shocker,[21] but the circulation of *Hampton's* was small, and Russell was soon on to other tasks. Generally speaking, it was the continuing series such as Ida Tarbell's Standard Oil history, Steffens's cities, Adams's patent medicine, and Baker's railroad and race relations stories that attracted the most attention.

Industrial strife did not gain the full attention of any of the muckrakers, although headlines and legislative investigations gave ample indication that this was the most violent period in the history of the Republic. Organized labor was something that never seemed quite explicable when rendered through the middle-class values of many of the journalists. C.P. Connolly blamed capital more than labor for the bitter outbreaks in the West, but he believed that "Big Bill" Haywood and Clarence Darrow, who had been a lawyer for the Los Angeles *Times* dynamiters, had escaped imprisonment only through a defective legal system. Ray Stannard Baker reported the widespread strike violence in Colorado wherein a society-wide conspiracy to break laws resulted in dynamiting, illegal military force, scab-beatings, arrests without warrants, violation of habeas corpus, and biased judges, all stemming from the lawlessness of union bludgeons and capital's anarchy by finesse.[22] But for the role and corruption of the law in industrial war, the muckrakers offered no systemic analyses or solutions outside of Steffens's golden rule and Sinclair's socialism.

There was, however, one vital area where a muckraker led rather than followed educated concern about the failure of the law. Ray Stannard Baker's articles on the Atlanta Riot of 1906 and his *Following the Color Line* series were a unique and far-reaching factual argument that justice in America was not for the black. Baker has been fairly criticized by recent commentators, as well as some black leadership of his time, for his compromises, stereotyping, and lack of commitment to immediate change.[23] It is accurate to say that he favored Booker T. Washington's accommodationism to DuBois' equal-rightism, accepted segregation in transportation, and lent support to racial stereotyping in telling of "low" and "criminal" types. At the same time, he offered repeated testimony of the failure to provide either protection or justice for the Negro, and he documented what we would today characterize as the "institutional racism" of the justice-delivery systems, North and South. He described how the police terrorized Negroes, lawyers exploited or ignored them, and the law and judiciary supported the cruel and exploitative labor systems of "debt slavery" or peonage, the chain gang, and contract labor.

"One thing impressed me especially," he wrote, "not only in this court but in all others I have visited: A Negro brought in for drunkenness, for example, was punished more severely than a white man arrested for the same offense. The injustice which the weak everywhere suffer—North and South—is in the South visited upon the Negro. The white man sometimes escaped with a reprimand, he was sometimes fined three dollars and costs, but the Negro, especially if he had no white man to intercede for him, was usually punished with a ten or fifteen dollar fine, which often meant that he must go to the chain-gang. One of the chief causes of complaint by the Negroes of Atlanta has been of the rough treatment of the police and of unjust arrests."[24]

Baker particularly attributed lynching to a general lack of faith in the criminal-justice system. Although he gave much credit to the press and tradition in producing the racial hysteria that led to violence, Baker offered an institutional explanation. In every lynch town, he reported, weakness of the judicial system produced the widespread contempt for the law which resulted in the lynch mob. Lynch towns all had bad records for homicide, justice, and regard for the sacredness of human life. This condition prevailed in the North as well as the South. Madison County, Alabama, was not that different from Springfield, Ohio, where he reported that the soil had been "richly prepared" for the occurrence of its lynching by "corrupt politics, vile saloons, the law paralysed by non-

enforcement against vice, a large venal Negro vote, lax courts of justice."
Danville, East St. Louis, and Chicago were no better.

Although he reported the efforts of sometimes courageous judges, grand juries, and sheriffs, and some signs of hope as in the Indianapolis juvenile court and probation system, he held the white man accountable for justice and order. "If the white man sets an example of non-obedience to law, of non-enforcement of law, of unequal justice, what can be expected of the Negro?"[25]

Despite a tendency to refer to "criminal-type" blacks and to use the kind of metaphor that unwittingly conveyed a biological view of racial behavior, Baker overtly argued the other way. Collectively, the muckrakers rejected the idea of racial inferiority and its corollary that criminality and high crime rates could be particularly blamed on the Negro or immigrant. As Steffens had shown in writing of Philadelphia and Rhode Island, corruption was as native to old-stock American cities as it was to the newer immigrant ones. Baker, Russell, and the rest attributed criminality to the lack of education and opportunity and to an exploitative environment. "The records of murders and homicides in various countries seem to show," S.S. McClure had argued in 1904, "that foreigners in the United States acquire most of their disrespect for law after they come among us."[26]

In summary, the journalists of exposure filled a decade's worth of the popular magazines with detailed accounts of national "lawlessness," touching almost all aspects of American life. At the same time, they evidenced, for the most part, little knowledge of the subcultures and functioning of the justice-delivery system. They peered into the streets, the police stations, the courts, and penal systems but seem not to have mastered the inner life of any of them. It is not possible to blame all of this on their middle-class status and innocence. C.P. Connolly had been a lawyer and a prosecutor; many of the journalists had served their apprenticeships as police reporters, and Lincoln Steffens, perhaps better than anyone else of his time, knew his way around in both criminal and police circles.

What shaped their views of everything else was the concentrated and practically unchecked economic power which had developed in America, and to this, in various ways, they related the "lawlessness." From this central concern, which was the core of progressivism, the journalists of exposure poked into practically every corner of society. This is what Louis Filler showed in his *Crusaders for American Liberalism*, which will always be the seminal work on the muckrakers and their world. In it he described not only the extent of their search for what was wrong in

America, but also the excitement that exploration contained. As Filler summed it up, writing of 1910, muckraking was "free, virile, and aggressive."[27] Its concern was, in varying degrees for each of the journalists, the conflict between an economic motivation and economic system and the civic values which they identified with democracy. It was—and is—a serious problem, and one which led at least the muckraker socialists to despair of both systems.

What all the muckrakers tended to miss was a full appreciation of the separate interests and life of the justice-delivery system, which responds to the dominant forces in society and also operates within a world of its own. It can make its own contribution to the failure of justice, in addition to and apart from the influence of those other conflicts which the muckrakers described as corruption and the lawlessness of capital. And when the justice system goes astray, it may well compromise the legitimacy of the larger society as well.

Notes

1. *The Challenge of Crime in a Free Society* (Washington, 1967), pp. vii, 12.

2. Dealing only with the state courts, James's eleven categories are: the hacks, the retirees, the failures, the inattentive, the misfits, the informal, the incapacitated, the inexperienced, the lazy, the weak, and the prejudiced. See Howard James, *Crisis in the Courts* (reprint, New York, 1968), pp. 6–7. James goes on to find the whole system producing something seriously less than justice. See also James S. Campbell, Joseph R. Sahid, and David P. Stang, *Law and Order Reconsidered* (Washington, 1969), chaps. 3, 13–24.

3. *The Challenge of Crime in a Free Society*, pp. 7–10, 14, 93.

4. S.S. McClure, "The Increase of Lawlessness in the United States," *McClure's*, 24 (1904), 163–71; "One Cause for Increase of Crime," *Outlook*, 84 (1906), 106–8; "Crime and Capital Punishment: A Symposium," *Annals of the American Academy*, 29 (1907), 601–3; Charles A. Ellwood, "Has Crime Increased in the United States Since 1880?" *Journal of the American Institute of Criminal Law and Criminology*, 1 (1910), 378–85; William D. Miller, *Memphis During the Progressive Era* (Memphis, 1957), chap. 5.

5. James E. Cutler, *Lynch-Law* (New York, 1905), p. 1; Charles Crowe, "Racial Violence and Social Reform—Origins of the Atlanta Riot of 1906," *Journal of Negro History*, 53 (1968), 234–56; Philip Taft and Philip Ross, "American Labor Violence: Its Causes, Character, and Outcome," in *The History of Violence in America*, edited by H.D. Graham and T.R. Gurr (New York, 1969), chap. 8; Graham Adams, *Age of Industrial Violence* (New York, 1966); Theodore N. Ferdinand, "The Criminal Patterns of Boston Since 1849," *American Journal of Sociology*, 73 (1967), 84–99.

6. William H. Taft, "Delays and Defects in the Enforcement of Law in This Country," *North American Review*, 187 (1908), 851.

7. Roscoe Pound, "The Causes of Popular Dissatisfaction with the Administration of Justice," (29 *ABA Rep.* 395, Part I, 1906); *Journal of Criminal Law, Criminology, and Police Science*, Vols. 1–3; *The American Yearbook*, 1910–1912; Reginald H. Smith, *Justice and the Poor* (New York, 1917); Felix Frankfurter and James M. Landis, *The Business of the Supreme Court* (New York, 1928), chaps. 3–4.

8. *McClure's*, 20 (1903), 336.

9. See Stanley K. Schultz, "The Morality of Politics: The Muckrakers' Vision of Democracy," *Journal of American History*, 52 (1965), 527–47.

10. Ray Stannard Baker, Notebook C, p. 46. MS. Ray Stannard Baker Papers (Library of Congress); Will Irwin, "They Who Strife in the Dark," *American*, 67 (1909), 564.

11. *McClure's*, 24 (1904), 163–71.

12. Samuel Hopkins Adams, in *Ridgway's I* (Oct. 6, 1906), 4–5; (Oct. 27, 1906), 7; (Nov. 3, 1906), 8; (Nov. 24, 1906), 9; (Dec. 1, 1906), 9; (Dec. 8, 1906), 9; David Graham Phillips, *The Plum Tree* (Indianapolis, 1905); Upton Sinclair, *The Jungle* (New York, 1906); Charles Edward Russell, *The Greatest Trust in the World* (New York, 1905) and *Why I Am a Socialist* (New York, 1910); Gustavus Myers, *History of the Supreme Court of the United States* (Chicago, 1912).

13. Samuel Hopkins Adams, "What Has Become of Our Pure Food Law?" *Hampton's*, 24 (1910), 242; Cf, also *Ridgway's*, October 1906–February 1907.

14. Ray Stannard Baker, Notebook J., 128–33, Baker Papers. Cf. also "Railroads on Trial," *McClure's*, 26 (1906), 326; John E. Semonche, *Ray Stannard Baker* (Chapel Hill, 1969), pp. 142–47; Robert S. Maxwell, "A Note on the Muckrakers," *Mid-America*, 43 (1961), 55–60.

15. *Collier's*, 48 (Dec. 23, 1911), 21.

16. C.P. Connolly, "Big Business and the Bench," *Everybody's*, 26 (1912), 146–60, 291–306; 439–53; 659–72; 827–41; 27 (1912), 116–28; "More Loopholes," *Collier's*, 42 (Feb. 20, 1909), 9; "Protest by Dynamite," *Collier's*, 48 (1912), 9–10.

17. Carl Snyder, *Collier's*, 48 (Nov. 25, 1911), 15–16, 25; (Dec. 2, 1911), 19–20, 34, 35; (Dec. 23, 1911), 7–8, 21; (Dec. 30, 1911), 11–12; 49 (Jan. 6, 1912), 19–20, 30; (Feb. 10, 1912), 11–12; (Feb. 24, 1912), 11–12, 27, 28.

18. Carl Snyder, *Collier's*, 48 (Dec. 2, 1911), 35.

19. S.H. Adams, "The New York Police Forces," *Collier's*, 39 (March 30, 1907), 15–17; G.K. Turner, "The City of Chicago," *McClure's*, 28 (1907), 575–92; "Tammany's Control of New York by Professional Criminals," *McClure's*, 33 (1909), 117–34; "Daughters of the Poor," *McClure's* 34 (1909), 45–61; "Traders in Women," *Harper's Weekly*, 62 (June 21, 1913), 11; also unsigned editorials *McClure's*, 35 (1910), 346–48, 471–73; 36 (1910), 122; Upton Sinclair, *The Jungle* (New York, 1906), pp. 17–18, 302–3; Lincoln Steffens, *The Shame of the Cities* (New York, 1904); for Josiah Flynt, see Louis Filler, *Crusaders for American Liberalism* (New York, 1939), chap. VI. For an excellent recent analysis of urban politics, crime, and justice, see Mark H. Haller, "Urban Crime and Criminal Justice: The Chicago Case," *Journal of American History*, 57 (1970), 619–35.

20. Lincoln Steffens, *Upbuilders* (New York, 1909), pp. 94–243.

21. Charles Edward Russell, "A Burglar in the Making," *Everybody's*, 18 (1908), 753–60; "Beating Men to Make Them Good," *Hampton's*, 23 (1909), 312–23, 484–96, 609–20.

22. C.P. Connolly, "The Moyer-Haywood Case," *Collier's*, 39 (May 11, 1907), 13–15, (May 18, 1907), 21–22, (May 25, 1907), 23, (June 22, 1907), 11–12, (June 29, 1907), 15–17, 28–29, (July 6, 1907), 11–13, (July 20, 1907), 13–14, (July 27, 1907), 13–14; "A Little Drama Out in Idaho," *Collier's*, 40 (Dec. 7, 1907), 19–20;

"Pettibone and Sheriff Brown," *Collier's*, 40 (Jan. 25, 1908), 11–13; "The Trial at Los Angeles," *Collier's*, 48 (Oct. 14, 1911), 17, 31, 32; "The Saving of Clarence Darrow," *Collier's*, 48 (Dec. 23, 1911), 9–10; "Protest by Dynamite," *Collier's*, 48 (Jan. 13, 1912), 9–10; Ray Stannard Baker, "The Reign of Lawlessness," *Mc-Clure's*, 23 (1904), 43–57.

23. Robert C. Bannister, "Ray Stannard Baker's *Following the Color Line*: Jim Crow and White Progressives," paper presented at the American Historical Association meetings, Washington, D.C., 1969; Herbert Shapiro, "The Muckrakers and the Negroes," *Phylon*, 31 (1970), 76–88; Charles Crowe, "Racial Massacre in Atlanta, September 22, 1906," *J. Negro Hist.*, 54 (1969), 170–71.

24. Ray Stannard Baker, *Following the Color Line* (New York, 1908), p. 49.

25. Ibid., pp. 182–83, 205, 215.

26. *McClure's*, 24 (1904), 171.

27. Louis Filler, *Crusaders for American Liberalism*, p. 341.

At no time in American history has the relationship between literature and journalism been so close as it was during the period when muckraking was at its height. Many of the most active muckrakers crossed the line between the two with some regularity; others moved deliberately from one to the other at some stage in their lives; still others entertained ambitions toward a literary career, but settled for journalism as a more remunerative and rewarding way of expressing themselves.

It can be persuasively argued that there was a particular similarity between the literature and the journalism of a period extending from the late nineteenth century through most of the first two decades of the twentieth. In the realism and naturalism that pervaded the fiction of those years, there were close relationships with the new journalism that characterized the newspapers of Joseph Pulitzer, William Randolph Hearst, and E.W. Scripps, and—a few years later—the popular magazines that provided a forum for the muckrakers.

Increasing numbers of the American novelists after the Civil War had begun to write as journalists. Born in the Jacksonian era, when the popular press burgeoned, they had been apprenticed to the printing trade, had been schooled in writing for newspapers, and had eventually turned to literature—with varying degrees of success. Mark Twain is only the most notable among many such writers.

Then, as the influences of realism and naturalism reached across the Atlantic from Europe, the relationship between journalism and literature was intensified. Many a young man whose ambition was to write novels saw reporting for newspapers as the best way to learn about that "real world" he would later depict in literary forms. So it was that Frank Norris, Stephen Crane, Theodore Dreiser, and many others began as journalists, seeking the kinds of first-hand experiences they believed were needed to enable them to create the fiction they wanted to write. Whether the novels and short stories they did write were "muckraking fiction"—as they have sometimes been described—is of less than primary concern. What is important is that they represent a particular aspect of the relationship between the journalism and the literature of their time.

A more typical muckraking novelist was David Graham Phillips, who, having become a journalist after his graduation from Princeton, turned to writing fiction with the deliberate purpose of accomplishing through his novels what others were seeking to do in the muckraking magazines. Phillips was, in fact, already launched on a career of great promise with Pulitzer's *World* when he deliberately severed his journalistic connections and began writing novels, which he saw as the most effective way to reach a large audience.

Some would certainly argue that Phillips might better have stuck with journalism and—more specifically—with the muckraking writers for the popular magazines of his time. He is best remembered today for his "Treason of the Senate" series, published in Hearst's *Cosmopolitan* magazine in 1906. His novels—with the possible exception of the posthumously published *Susan Lenox*—have generally been dismissed by critics as having slight merit. And the "message novel"—intended to stir public concern and action—has fallen on bad times in critical circles in recent years, though such novels continue to do well in the best-seller lists.

Is there, then, a place for muckraking in literature? Both John Cawelti and Jay Martin, in the essays which follow, suggest that there is, though each is careful to define literature broadly enough to avoid the allegation that he is attributing literary merit to the novels cited in support of his contention.

Even, so, the Cawelti paper in particular has been the object of much indignation and outrage among those who heard it and others who have since read it. Is he really suggesting that the so-called "blockbuster" novels of Harold Robbins, Jacqueline Susann, and many others represent an extension of the muckraking impulse in our own times? Is he comparing these purveyors of sensation with such honored figures as Lincoln Steffens, Ida Tarbell, or even David Graham Phillips?

Quite clearly he is, though not in a direct way and though some of the nuances of his thinking obviously escaped those who were so disturbed. For what both Cawelti and Martin do suggest is that literature (broadly defined) has long been, and continues to be, a favorite means of serving the general purposes of muckracking. The contemporary novels they discuss may have neither great literary merit nor high purpose, but they are clearly intended to expose social conditions and situations to a public that is curious about such problems.

The key to an understanding of what both are saying is to be found in the contention—which each states clearly and reaffirms several times— that the mukraking impulse in literature has been appropriated in recent years by popular culture. It has been perverted and exploited to serve quite different purposes from those the earlier users of it intended it to serve. Where Phillips and, to a lesser extent, Dreiser, Norris, and

Crane wrote muckraking novels to arouse the public to action against evils and abuses in the society and its institutions, those contemporary novelists who have appropriated what Martin describes as the "muckraking aesthetic" have used it to entertain and titillate the public, thus serving their own commercial purposes. Or, in Cawelti's words, "instead of confronting their readers with the shortcomings of the social structure, the blockbusters use muckraking for purposes of entertainment and escape."

Martin does conclude on an optimistic note—or, at least, a hopeful one—when he suggests that "we need the muckraking analysts and the novelists," just as we have needed them before. Of the muckraking writers of earlier times, he suggests that "our modern world, the seventies, is what they were all the while making for and meaning," and concludes that "if they once moved our minds or hearts, they can do so again, and so move us into our future."

Whether or not one recognizes the muckraking impulse in some of the novels discussed by Cawelti and Martin, or whether one agrees with their mutual contention that the muckraking novel has become a part of the popular culture from which it may be reclaimed by serious writers, there is much in their contributions that will be useful to those who contemplate the future of muckraking in either its literary or its journalistic forms.

Blockbusters and Muckraking

Some Reflections on Muckraking in the Contemporary Best-Seller

John G. Cawelti

In recent years, we have increasingly come to think of muckraking as a rather short-lived, passing phase of American literature and culture. For example, Jay Martin, in his book *Harvests of Change,* suggests that muckraking was a rather confused emotional response to a number of middleclass discontents at the turn of the century and that it rapidly ran its course.

> From 1901 to about 1912, the literature of exposure dominated the middle-class imagination by giving the vague feelings of hostility and frustration a focus in the evils of the new metropolitanism. By 1914 the formula of exposure had hardened into a stereotype and inured the public to revelations of corruption, no matter how sensational. David Graham Phillips and others had begun to rely upon emotional rather than documentary exposures by using mysterious and magical phrases like "the system," "the interests," and "the syndicates." By 1914, this had gone so far that even Mr. Dooley was satirizing the corruption of "the McClure gang." Then, too, around this time returning prosperity

for the middle class made progress look more likely than poverty and quieted the fears that had given exposure its compelling emotional appeal.[1]

I cannot quarrel with most of this statement. The journalism of exposure as practiced in this period by writers like Ida Tarbell, Lincoln Steffens, Ray Stannard Baker, and Jacob Riis, along with fictional muckraking like Upton Sinclair's *The Jungle* (1906), David Graham Phillips's *The Great God Success* (1901) and *Susan Lenox* (1917), and Theodore Dreiser's *Sister Carrie* (1900) and *The Financier* (1912), belongs largely to the years from 1890 to the First World War. Indeed, the transitory flavor of this particular period comes out even more strongly in works lacking the artistic merit that gives most of the novels I have mentioned some claim to attention beyond their period. Thus, my favorite symbol of the muckraking novel is a work of which I believe I am safe in claiming to be the only living reader. It was published by an irate Chicagoan in 1885 and I cherish it because its title sums up so much of the muckraking ethos. This immortal gem was called: *An Iron Crown or: The Modern Mammon: A Graphic and Thrilling History of Great Money-makers and How They Got Millions: Both Sides of the Picture—Railway Kings, Coal Barons, Bonanza Miners and Their Victims: Life and Adventure from Wall Street to the Rocky Mountains: Board of Trade Frauds, Bucket-Shop Frauds, Newspaper Frauds, All Sorts of Frauds, Big and Little.*[2]

However, though we define a fairly distinctive literature of muckraking limited to the years around the turn of the century, we should not forget that in a somewhat broader sense, muckraking has always been an element of the novel. The early picaresque tales of seventeenth-century England and Spain lovingly catalogued the hidden criminality beneath the surface of the social order. In the eighteenth century, novelists like Fielding and Defoe wrote novels unmasking roguery at all social levels. Of course, the satirical exposes of Fielding differed substantially from later nineteenth-century muckraking. For example, the American muckrakers focused their attention on institutions and the social structure, and their purpose was not primarily ridicule, but reform. Therefore they were much more concerned about verisimilitude and documentary accuracy in their portrayal of society than Fielding, whose target was generic human folly and not the particular shortcomings of social institutions.

But if novelists who expose the corruption of particular institutions are muckrakers we must surely recognize Charles Dickens as the creator of a novelistic form embodying this purpose. Dickens, of course, was not predominantly a satirist. In many of his novels he attacked and demanded the reform of such specific social institutions as the debtors' prisons, the poorhouses, and chancery law. Dickens was rapidly imported to America, as both a best-selling author and a major literary influence. Harriet Beecher Stowe, whose literary efforts certainly bore the Dickensian stamp, became America's first great novelistic muckraker. This Dickensian tradition of social criticism, centering around the analysis of particular institutions, was one of the mainstreams of the nineteenth-century novel in America. Twain and Warner's *The Gilded Age* raked the muck of American business and politics brought to the surface by such actual scandals as the Credit Mobilier. William Dean Howells and lesser writers like Henry B. Fuller continued the tradition in their novels of business and the city. *A Hazard of New Fortunes,* though easier on the stomach than *The Jungle,* nonetheless contains a trenchant analysis of the intersecting relationships of business, journalism, and philanthropy, not unlike the famous dissections of the interconnections of business, politics, and crime which Lincoln Steffens began to publish a few years later.

Thus, the muckraking novelists of the turn of the century, however much they developed their own "formula of exposure," grew out of a long tradition of social exposure in the novel. Strangely enough, muckraking does not at first glance seem to continue as an important stream in the later twentieth century. The major novelists of the twenties and thirties, with the important exception of Sinclair Lewis, turned away from muckraking. Faulkner and Hemingway abandoned the muckraker's specific social analysis and criticism in quest of a more universal understanding of human strengths and weaknesses. Others, like the proletarian novelists of the thirties, followed the classical muckraker Lincoln Steffens beyond the exposure of existing social corruption in search of a more radical vision of revolutionary social transformation. Today, those writers who appear to be our most significant novelists—Saul Bellow, Bernard Malamud, John Updike, John Barth, Joseph Heller, Thomas Pynchon, Ralph Ellison, James Baldwin, Philip Roth—show much more concern with metaphysics than with muckraking, with individual dilemmas than with institutional exposes.

Is muckraking dead then? Not at all. Like many things that originally appeared in our culture as instruments of protest, muckraking has been captured by the institutions of mass entertainment, and has become big business. If we look at that group of writers who create those enormous, immensely popular, best-selling fictions which are invariably merchandised as "blockbusters"—the sprawling, panoramic social romances of writers like Harold Robbins, Irving Wallace, Arthur Hailey, Jacqueline Susann, Henry Sutton, and many others—we find that in many aspects of structure and theme they are the lineal descendants of the muckraking novelists of the turn of the century.

Classical muckraking used fictional form to expose the contrast between public beliefs about American society and the actual realities of power and corruption beneath the surface. The muckrakers brought out what purported to be the inside story of the stock market, the meatpacking industry, the drug industry, the Standard Oil Corporation, the publishing industry, etc. This behind-the-scenes approach to major American institutions is one of the principal claims of the blockbuster and, to judge from the advertising blurbs which stress this aspect of the novels, a prime source of its audience appeal. Mario Puzo's *The Godfather,* a recent best-seller, is "the sensational blockbuster of a novel that everyone is talking about . . . the most revealing novel ever written about the criminal underworld of the mafia." Harold Robbins's *The Dream Merchants* is a "sensational, behind-the-scene story of the motion picture business." A few other samples: "the inside story of the modeling business"; "the uncensored personal story behind a national sex survey"; "the stark, behind-the-scenes novel of a big city police department"; "the sensational novel that blows the lid off the international film community . . . the secret lives of its rich, talented, beautiful people . . . and the meteoric rise of a young actress who cooperated fully in the corruption of her own innocence"; "this novel—big, brilliant, savage and sensational—tells its inside story . . . the shockingly true story behind those headlines."[3]

Secondly, the classical muckraking novels and the contemporary blockbusters have many subjects in common. In *Peyton Place* and its varied progeny the small town is raked over in a way similar to the first part of Phillips's *Susan Lenox* or Lewis's *Main Street.* One standard blockbuster character, the girl who seeks to escape from the narrow frustrations and petty hypocrisies of middle-class small-town life by seeking glamour and excitement in the cities, might be considered the daughter or granddaughter of Phillips's Susan Lenox, Dreiser's Sister Carrie, and Lewis's Carol Kennicott. Like the muckrakers the writers of blockbusters delight in showing us the corruptions and hidden pressures beneath the respectable facade of our major political and economic institutions. Thus, *The God-*

father shows how much influence the Mafia has over the courts, the police, and many businesses in the United States; Harold Robbins specializes in the sensational sexual peculiarities which influence major figures in the entertainment business and the jet set; *The Chapman Report* reveals the confused sexual lives of the upper-middle-class residents of an elite suburbia; *Advise and Consent* uncovers the naked ambitions, the hidden schemes, and the unscrupulous and reckless tactics which shape the political process in the U.S. Senate; *The Voyeur* deals with the personal ambitions and animosities which lie behind a supposedly moralistic political crusade against the publisher of a sexy magazine.

It is strange that muckraking, once associated with movements of political and social reform, should now be a major stock in trade of the best-seller. I intend to make a preliminary exploration of this paradox by, first, defining more precisely what happens to the techniques and ideas of the muckrakers when they become part of the craft of the popular entertainer. Then, with this relationship more sharply in view, I will suggest some of the reasons why muckraking now plays a central role in best-selling popular novels.

Both classical muckrakers and blockbuster writers tend to work with panoramic social settings in which many characters are involved. These settings are heavy with documentation. Though often given fictional names, the settings are developed with a specificity that constantly reminds the reader of their correspondence with real locales and institutions. This documentary quality is important in establishing the sense that the novel is about social reality and that it is an accurate and full report of that reality. In addition, both muckrakers and blockbusters treat their setting in such a way as to give the reader the sense that he is being taken behind the scenes and shown a reality that is normally hidden from public view.

However, once we have stated these important similarities some fundamental differences immediately become clear. First of all, one of the primary milieus of the muckraking novel is almost entirely missing from the blockbuster, that of the urban poor. In Upton Sinclair's *The Jungle* the entire novel centers around the desperate struggle of immigrant workers in the Chicago meat-packing industry. About a third of Phillips's *Susan Lenox* deals with the heroine's experiences as an urban worker in factories and sweatshops: another third narrates her life as a prostitute in the seamy world of commercial vice. The same pattern holds true for Dreiser's *Sister Carrie*. In the blockbuster, however, the milieu of urban poverty is almost entirely missing. While blockbuster writers occasionally give us a flashback to the early struggles of their characters, the focus of our attention is the world of affluence, power, glamour, and excitement.

Though the affluent world is a place of glamour and excitement, it is also the source of corruption and unhappiness. In contrast to this, blockbuster writers often sentimentalize or romanticize the small-town or lower-class origins of their characters, in a way that runs almost exactly counter to the treatment of poverty and the small town by the classical muckrakers. Indeed, this practice resembles that sentimental popular tradition in American literature which Sinclair Lewis ironically summarized in this passage from *Main Street*:

> In reading popular stories and seeing plays, asserted Carol, she had found only two traditions of the American small town. The first tradition, repeated in scores of magazines every month, is that the American village remains the one sure abode of friendship, honesty, and clean sweet marriageable girls. Therefore all men who succeed in painting in Paris or in finance in New York at last become weary of smart women, return to their native towns, assert that cities are vicious, marry their childhood sweethearts and, presumably, joyously abide in those towns until death.[4]

This formulation is a little too simple to fit the majority of the blockbuster novels. Coming from a later age, many have absorbed the platitude, "you can't go home again." Thus, characters often discover rather sadly that the glamorous world has failed them, but that they cannot return to the simpler milieu in which they might have found happiness. This, for example, is the final state of Anne Welles, one of the heroines of *Valley of the Dolls*. Nonetheless, it is surprising how much the value of the simpler nonurban life persists as an article of faith in the blockbuster. The heroine of *The Beauty Trap*—an expose of the modeling business and an obvious attempt to duplicate the success of Jacqueline Susann's novels of the glamour world—finally arrives at the realization that the city is a trap she must flee in search of freedom and integrity:

> Eve smiled, grateful her life had come this present route. The city lay behind her now. The odor of the Secaucus garbage dumps only a few minutes ahead would be like the scent of heaven, bringing her to the Jersey Turnpike and onward—to the unknown, the uncharted. Her heart sang, I'm free, I'm myself, and I have faith, the faith to believe in what lies ahead.[5]

The presence in the blockbusting world of areas of decency and good-ness which have somehow not been touched by the pervasive corruption is another important difference in the treatment of milieu. In this respect, the blockbusters resemble such premuckraking novels of social criticism as those of Dickens, or Twain and Warner's *The Gilded Age*. In *Bleak House*, the contrast between the corruption and misery which emanates like a choking fog from Chancery Court and the clean lucid decency of Bleak House is raised to a level of high artistry by Dickens's great power of symbolic imagination. Twain and Warner attempted to use the same kind of contrast as an organizing principle of *The Gilded Age*, by setting the story of the Hawkins family and its increasing involvement in political and social corruption against the Horatio-Alger-like subplot of the ro-mance and success of Philip Sterling and Ruth Bolton. Even *An Iron Crown, or the Modern Mammon* contrasts the goodness and decency of the small towns and rural areas with the corruption of the cities. Indeed the author of that novel cries out against the danger of chicanery and fraud spreading out from the cities and destroying American democracy:

> God forbid that this monster of political corruption should ever crawl from his slimy den in our great cities to fasten on the honest rural dis-tricts. When he does so unrebuked, the grandest experiment ever tried of government by the people and for the people will be recorded in the book of time as a failure.[6]

In Sinclair, Phillips, and Dreiser, however, the contrast between cor-ruption and innocence is largely replaced by a view of total social corrup-tion caused by the capitalist system of exploitation, which has an influ-ence so pervasive that no areas of society are free from it. Rich and poor, sadistic and benevolent, urban and rural—all are trapped by the web of exploitation. As the socialist speaker puts it at the end of *The Jungle*:

> I am here to plead with you, to know if want and misery have yet done their work with you, if injustice and oppression have yet opened your eyes! I shall still be waiting—there is nothing else that I can do. There is no wilderness where I can hide from these things, there is no haven where I can escape them; though I travel to the ends of the earth, I find the same accursed system—I find that all the fair and noble impulses of humanity, the dreams of poets and the agonies of martyrs, are shackled and bound in the service of organized and predatory greed.[7]

Or as Phillips puts it in *Susan Lenox,* it is impossible in the present social system to make a meaningful moral distinction between money earned through supposedly respectable pursuits and the income of corruption:

Anyone disposed to be critical of police and morality—or of Freddie Palmer [a gangster] morality—in this matter of graft would do well to pause and consider the source of his own income before he waxes too eloquent and too virtuous. Graft is one of those general words that mean everything and nothing. What is graft and what is honest income? Just where shall we draw the line between rightful exploitation of our fellow-beings through their necessities and their ignorance of their helplessness, and wrongful exploitation? Do attempts to draw that line resolve down to making virtuous whatever I may appropriate and making vicious whatever is appropriated in ways other than mine? And if so are not the police and the Palmers entitled to their day in the moral court no less than the tariff-baron and market-cornerer, the herder and driver of wage slaves, the retail artists in cold storage, filth, short weight and shoddy goods?[8]

True, the muckrakers had an unfortunate tendency to let the notion of the system become a purely emotional symbol of evil and a substitute for clear political and social distinctions. But their conception of society as a complete system of exploitation gave a kind of direction and force to their social criticism that is largely missing from the blockbusters. After reading *The Jungle* the American public was not converted to socialism as Upton Sinclair probably hoped, but it was ready to insist on the passage of pure food and drug legislation. One can hardly imagine any sort of legislation growing out of *Valley of the Dolls*, or *The Godfather*, or *The Carpetbaggers*, despite the exposures of corruption in high places so central to these novels.

What then is the nature of the evils which the blockbusting novelists so enthusiastically expose? Most importantly, the corruption which essentially interests them is personal rather than political. It is the result of human weaknesses rather than the faults of a particular social or political order. Even where the blockbuster has an explicitly political subject, such as Allen Drury's *Advise and Consent*, the evils exposed are caused by a combination of personal ambitions, past perversities, and present miscalculations, not by the nature of the institutional system. *Valley of the Dolls* is not an exposure of the way in which drug manufacturers profit from the exploitation of human needs, but an anatomization of the corrupting effects of individual greed and ambition. Only in one way do the blockbusters imply that corruption is the result of the structure of society rather than the product of human weaknesses. One of the central principles of the blockbuster world is the invariable corruption of an unchecked drive to power. As one character in *Valley of the Dolls* put it:

"In this rat race you whore, lie, cheat and use every trick you can employ to get up there where Henry is. This business demands it. And that's what I'm ranting against. Not Henry personally, but what everyone turns into if he sticks in it long enough."[9]

Like the muckrakers, the blockbusters worry a great deal about the apparent decline of American society and the gap between the ideals of democracy and the sordid realities of modern life. But where the muckrakers traced this decline to a basic social and political cause, the blockbusters see a wide variety of human weaknesses at work. One of the characters in *Advise and Consent* suggests that only the failures of everyone can account for the present situation:

A universal guilt enshrouded the middle years of the twentieth century in America; and it attached to all who participated in those times. It attached to the fatuous, empty-headed liberals who had made it so easy for the Russians by yielding them so much; it attached to the embittered conservatives who had closed the doors on human love and frozen out all possibility of communication between peoples. It rested on the military, who had been too jealous of one another and too slow, and on the scientists, who had been too self-righteous and irresponsible and smug about shifting the implications of what they did on to someone else, and on the press, which had been too lazy and too compliant in the face of evils foreign and domestic, and on the politicians who had been too self-interested and not true enough to the destiny of the land they had in keeping, and not least upon the ordinary citizen and his wife, who somehow didn't quite give enough of a damn about their country in spite of all their self-congratulatory airs about how patriotic they were. Nobody could stand forth now in America and say, "I am guiltless. I had no part in this. I did not help bring America down from her bright pinnacle."[10]

More commonly the blockbuster view of human weakness as the cause of corruption takes a form as simplified as the world-view of the muckrakers. Pauline Kael, in the course of a vigorous denunciation of the movie based on Harold Robbins's blockbuster *The Adventurers,* trenchantly summarizes the view of the world which runs through most of the blockbusters:

The movie is based on Robbins's law of eternal human corruption. The message is that nothing changes. The poor suffer and die, the rich are sated and empty, revolutionaries will be as bad as the oppressors they overturn, and so on. Everything is done by deals and corruption at the top, and nobody works for anything or takes any joy in accomplishment.[11]

Miss Kael fails to mention the important role of the realm of decency and goodness which can always save the characters from the eternal law of corruption, but insofar as her statement points to the fact that the blockbusters show little faith in individual or collective accomplishment and change, she is completely correct.

To sum up the major contrasts between the typical settings and subjects of the muckrakers and the blockbusters: First, the blockbusters have shifted their attention from the milieu of urban poverty and industrial enterprise to the affluent world of various elites, particularly those in the upper levels of mass entertainment, politics, and the more glamorous modern enterprises like those surrounding the airplane. In line with change, the blockbusters deal primarily with those persons who exercise power and control wealth rather than with the poor and the struggling. Second, there has been a shift from the exposure of systematic political and social corruption caused by an evil social structure to the revelation of personal corruption caused by individual human weaknesses. It is interesting to note, in connection with this shift in emphasis, that the best-selling novels of Sinclair Lewis in the 1920s made a transition between muckraking as the attack on a particular system of institutions and muckraking as the revelation of widespread individual corruption. Toward the end of *Main Street* Carol Kennicott tries to sum up her perception of the cause of society's failure to make a decent and rich life possible for most individuals. Like the muckrakers she has come to believe that it is a fault of the institutional structure; but unlike them she views this structure not as the result of a particular system like capitalism, but as something so diffuse as to be almost beyond change or reform:

> And why, she began to ask, did she rage at individuals? Not individuals but institutions are the enemies, and they most afflict the disciples who the most generously serve them. They insinuate their tyranny under a hundred guises and pompous names such as Polite Society, the Family, the Church, Sound Business, the Party, the Country, the Superior White race; and the only defense against them, Carol beheld, is unembittered laughter.[12]

Another way in which we can define the similarities and differences between the classical muckrakers and the contemporary blockbusters is by their treatment of character and action: What do these writers use as the primary pattern of human events around which they structure their long and complex narratives? What do they see as the central lines of action which will most move their readers and best give point to their portrayal of life? Two central thematic actions or plot lines dominated the classical muckraking novels: one might be called the failure of success, and the other the fortunate fall.[13] Sometimes, as in novels like Phillips's *The Great God Success*, Herrick's *Memoirs of An American Citizen*, Dreiser's *The Financier*, and Cahan's *The Rise of David Levinsky*, the failure of success is the dominant theme; in other novels, like Phillips's *Susan Lenox*, the fortunate fall is central; works like Dreiser's *Sister Carrie* combine the two.

A novel organized around the failure of success presents the story of a character who struggles to achieve wealth, power, or fame, but who realizes upon achieving these goals that they are largely empty and meaningless to him because in the process of gaining them he has somehow lost his chance for happiness. Thus, at the end of the novel, the central character is rich and famous but lonely, alienated, and unhappy. The fortunate fall is an action in which a character is plunged into a situation of degradation and misery, but in the process comes to a new understanding of life, develops new strengths, and achieves a significant triumph in the end. Both of these thematic actions were used by the muckraking novelists as a means of exposing the faults of the social system. For example, Howard, the publisher protagonist of Phillips's *The Great God Success*, eventually becomes the American ambassador to Great Britain, but to achieve this goal the system has forced him to betray his convictions and lose his integrity. In Dreiser's *Sister Carrie* the social system dooms Carrie to a life of misery and poverty so long as she tries to retain her respectability. But once she has fallen, she discovers the inner strength and the realistic knowledge which enables her to succeed as an actress. In this novel, Dreiser combines the two thematic actions of the failure of success and the fortunate fall; though her fall makes a new life possible for Carrie, the more successful she becomes the more she senses something empty and hollow about her life. Thus, the social system forces a career of immorality upon the innocent young girl, and then denies her any sense of fulfillment when she does achieve success.

Interestingly, both these thematic actions play a central role in the blockbuster novels. The failure of success is a blockbuster favorite. These novels teem with lonely and despairing individuals of wealth and power.

Indeed, success and power are invariably accompanied by isolation and unhappiness.

> What was it that Peter had once said? "When you're boss, Johnny, you're on your own. You got no friends, only enemies. If people are nice to you you wonder what they want from you. . . . Being boss is a lonely thing, Johnny a lonely thing."[14]

The San Francisco chief of police in Ernest K. Gann's *Of Good and Evil* realizes the same thing.

> [The ordinary citizens] didn't have to give a damn about . . . any of the cruelties people were going to inflict on each other before this day was finished. They had no need to concern themselves with the fact that [the chief] was looking at them from his cage and envying them. I'll have to watch it, Hill thought. It's getting worse all the time. Wasn't there some way a chief could do his job without being so lonely.[15]

Even the successful ladies are not exempt from loneliness. Anne Welles of *Valley of the Dolls* sees it like this:

> She brushed her hair and freshened her makeup. She looked fine. She had Lyon, the beautiful apartment, the beautiful child, the nice career of her own, New York—everything she had ever wanted. And from now on, she could never be hurt badly. She could always keep busy during the day, and at night—the lonely ones—there were always the beautiful dolls for company. She'd take two of them tonight. Why not? After all, it was New Year's Eve.[16]

Finally, at the very pinnacle of power, the presidency of the United States, the note is the same:

> The Majority Leader felt for one wild second that he should turn and run, he was so close to the absolute essence of the American Presidency, in the presence of a dedication so severe, so lonely, and so terrible, so utterly removed from the normal morality that holds society together, that he should flee from it before the revelation proved too shattering.[17]

If the president is the very essence of loneliness, no wonder that the ordinary millionaire or important career woman should be sad and isolated.

However, the thematic action of the failure of success has very different implications in the blockbusting novel from those it had in the classical muckrakers' works. There it served to demonstrate in action the incapability of the present institutional system to enable even the most successful individuals to achieve happiness. In the absence of the systematic institutional criticism of the muckrakers, the failure of success tends instead to become evidence of something like a law of compensation related to the eternal law of corruption. Success carries its invariable penalties; power can be gained only at a terrible price; there is no real happiness in being truly outstanding, for the greater one becomes the more misery it entails. Since men are weak and prone to corruption, the price of power is misery.

There is a similar shift in the meaning of the fortunate fall. Here in brief summary is a typical blockbusting example of this thematic action, as related in Harold Robbins's *The Dream Merchants*. From the moment of their first meeting in 1908, Doris Kessler falls in love with Johnny Edge. But Johnny must enter the degrading hustle of the movie business, in the course of which he marries an international sex symbol who makes his life miserable before he is able to realize thirty years later in 1938 that Doris is truly the woman for him. This curious tale is indicative of the blockbuster's treatment of the fortunate fall. First of all, as a result of the fall, the character finally discovers something he has really known all along, a discovery which usually involves a return to traditional values. For example, Dax Xenos, the international playboy of *The Adventurers*, finally realizes that it is his childhood sweetheart, rather than the dazzling procession of wealthy and glamorous women he has known, who holds the true meaning of life for him. Irv Kane, the wealthy publisher of *Tomcat* magazine, discovers that it is not the free sex life his magazine has preached and that he has attempted to embody in his own life, but a traditional, monogamous romantic love that is the key to happiness. Paul Radford, hero of *The Chapman Report*, immerses himself in investigation of all the infinite varieties of sexual behavior only to discover that sex is meaningless without romantic love and domesticity. In other words, instead of initiating the character from innocence into knowledge, the fortunate fall, as treated in the blockbuster, brings the character back to innocence again. Instead of freeing the character from the limitations of conventional morality and giving him the ability to struggle against the system the blockbusting novel initiates the character back into an acceptance of the conventional morality.

These, then, are some of the central similarities and differences in setting, subject, and thematic action between the contemporary bestseller and the muckraking novels of the turn of the century. By looking at them we can hazard a few speculations as to how and why muckraking has become an important device of mass entertainment.

In general, the blockbuster novelists have created a narrative form which makes use of the techniques of fictional organization and social analysis pioneered by the muckrakers, without the attack on a particular institutional structure and the impetus toward reform which characterized the muckraking novels. Thus, while both blockbusters and muckrakers exploit the public fascination with the inside story of important institutions, the blockbusters present social and individual corruption as a result of inescapable human weaknesses. Thereby the reader is helped to sympathize with and accept corruption rather than be disturbed by it. Moreover, the reader is enabled to see his own position outside the higher spheres of power and affluence as better and happier than that of the lonely elites who have succeeded in rising into the glamorous world of fame and fortune. The documentary realism which the muckrakers used to direct their readers' attention to the sufferings of the poor and the need for changes in the institutional structure is transformed by the blockbusters into a means of catering to an interest in the true story behind the public image of famous celebrities and a fascination with how institutions actually work. Most of the blockbusters are *romans a clef*; they are fictional versions of the lives of well-known celebrities so thinly disguised that readers can easily recognize them. Of course, this practice was not unheard-of in the earlier muckraking novel, since Dreiser based the character of Frank Cowperwood on Charles Yerkes. But there is an important difference. When the muckrakers based their novels on actual figures it was to demonstrate how their careers symbolized the characteristics of the institutional structure which produced them. The blockbusters, on the other hand, create highly fictionalized versions of their celebrity models in order to demonstrate that behind the public veneer of power or fame, so-and-so was actually a frail, lonely human being who needed love. In this way the reader is not only given the thrill of inside dope on a major figure, but also reassured that the colorless but decent life of the average middle classes is really happier after all.

The same sort of pattern emerges in the blockbuster treatment of institutions. First, practical details of institutional functioning presented without any critical animus occupy page after page of the blockbuster novel. Just what activities go on in the offices, kitchens, and basements of a luxury hotel? What are the procedures by which a presidential appointment is handled by the U.S. Senate? How does a police department function? Just what does a press agent do? How is the mafia organized and how does it arrange for a "hit"? What are the procedures by which a sex survey is carried out? Along with this how-to-do-it interest, the blockbuster treatment of institutions tends to reassure rather than to criticize, to justify rather than to call for change. It argues implicitly that the widespread effects of human weakness and corruption require the control of strong, responsible traditional institutions. Thus, for all its ambiguities, the U.S. Senate turns out to be a thoroughly responsible and benevolent institution, as Allen Drury portrays it in *Advise and Consent*. It is interesting to compare this with Phillips's sensational muckraking series "The Treason of the Senate." Even more strikingly, we are encouraged to take something of the same view of the Mafia in Puzo's recent best-seller, *The Godfather*, where, despite its tactics of murder, political corruption, and organized vice, the Corleone family in this dark Sicilian Bonanza suggests a contemporary Cartwright family striking out from its urban ranch in Long Island to eliminate anarchistic villains and bring about peace and harmony in the underworld. Indeed, in certain passages of that novel one detects a middle-class suburban fantasy of how life in America really ought to be carried out if only our social and political institutions were strong enough to bring about law and order:

> As soon as the Corleone Family set up their usual business liaison with the local police force they were informed of all such complaints and all crimes by professional criminals. In less than a year Long Beach became the most crime-free town of its size in the United States. Professional stickup artists and strong-arms received one warning not to ply their trade in the town. They were allowed one offense. When they committed a second they simply disappeared. The flim-flam home-improvement gyp artists, the door-to-door con men were politely warned that they were not welcome in Long Beach. Those confident con men who disregarded the warning were beaten within an inch of their lives. Resident young punks who had no respect for law and proper authority were advised in the most fatherly fashion to run away from home. Long Beach became a model city.[18]

Thus, instead of confronting their readers with the shortcomings of the social structure, the blockbusters use muckraking for purposes of entertainment and escape. By skillfully combining the sensational exposure of corruption in the lives of the great and notorious, and the fascination of glimpses into the inner workings of important social institutions with a basic framework of reassurance and reaffirmation of conventional middle-class values and institutions, the blockbuster novelists ease their sense of disorientation and danger in the complex world of the mid-twentieth century and feed that attitude toward social and political reality which David Riesman once characterized so trenchantly as inside-dopesterism:

> The inside-dopester may be one who has concluded. . . . that since he can do nothing to change politics, he can only understand it. Or he may see all political issues in terms of being able to get some insider on the telephone. That is, some inside-dopesters actually crave to *be* on the inside, to join an inner circle or invent one; others aim no higher than to *know* the inside, for whatever peer-group satisfactions this can bring them.[19]

Notes

1. Jay Martin, *Harvests of Change* (Englewood Cliffs, N.J., 1967), pp. 246–47.

2. An analysis of this work can be found in my earlier essay "Changing Ideas of Social Reform," *Social Service Review* 35 (1961), 282–87.

3. All these quotations are from the jackets of various blockbuster novels.

4. Sinclair Lewis, *Main Street* (New York, 1948), p. 263.

5. Jeanne Rejaunier, *The Beauty Trap* (New York, 1970), p. 406.

6. T.S. Denison, *An Iron Crown* (Chicago, 1885), p. 57.

7. Upton Sinclair, *The Jungle* (1906; reprint New York, 1960), p. 297.

8. David Graham Phillips, *Susan Lenox* (1917; reprint, Upper Saddle River, N.J., 1968), II, 174.

9. Jacqueline Susann, *Valley of the Dolls* (New York, 1967), pp. 179–80.

10. Allen Drury, *Advise and Consent* (1959; paperback, New York, 1961), p. 33.

11. Pauline Kael, "Scavengers with Computers," *The New Yorker* 46 (1970), 162.

12. Sinclair Lewis, *Main Street*, p. 430.

13. I am indebted to an unpublished ms. by Alan Rose entitled "Sin and the City: Urban Complexity and the Fortunate Fall in the American Success Novel" for helping me see the fortunate fall as a central thematic action in the muckraking novel; for further comments on the failure of success see my *Apostles of the Self-Made Man* (Chicago, 1965), pp. 227–36.

14. Harold Robbins, *The Dream Merchants* (1949; reprint, New York, 1961), p. 8.

15. Ernest K. Gann, *Of Good and Evil* (1963; reprint, New York, 1970), p. 134.

16. Jacqueline Susann, *Valley of the Dolls,* p. 500.

17. Allen Drury, *Advise and Consent*, p. 475.

18. Mario Puzo, *The Godfather* (New York, 1969), pp. 227–28.

19. David Riesman, *The Lonely Crowd* (Garden City, N.Y., 1955), p. 210.

The Literature of Argument and the Arguments of Literature

The Aesthetics of Muckraking

Jay Martin

In March of 1906, a month before President Theodore Roosevelt gave muckraking its name, Edwin E. Slosson, the editor of *The Independent*, undertook an assessment of what he called "The Literature of Exposure." "Fifty years from now," he prophesied, "when the historian of American literature writes of the opening of this century, he will give one of his most interesting chapters to the literature of exposure, and he will pronounce it a true intellectual force, a vital element in the creative activities of later years." He spoke of the rapidity and force with which muckraking had seized hold of the American imagination. But, he concluded, "It will disappear as quickly as it came."[1]

Slosson was certainly right: Muckraking virtually ceased by the end of the decade. By 1914, everyone agreed with President Wilson's remark to Congress that as a consequence of exposure, "at last the masters of business . . . have begun to yield their preference to their purpose, and perhaps their judgment also, in honorable surrender,"[2] still, muckraking had already become past history. By the 1920s, the muckraking movement seemed to offer merely one more instance of the failure of American social critics to understand the complexity of modern industrial and social systems. The reaction against muckraking began early and continued into the 1930s. In *Drift and Mastery*, published the year that Wilson spoke, Walter Lippmann argued that muckrakers, in misunderstanding modern technological change, had exposed abuses without attacking their causes in the nature of industry itself; in the twenties his criticisms were echoed by Vernon Louis Parrington and in the thirties by John Chamberlain.

Of course, the literature of exposure and the problems involved in judging it were hardly new as elements in American life. In "Man the Reformer," an address of 1841, Ralph Waldo Emerson noted the currency of a "general inquisition into abuses," and asserted that "in the history of the world the doctrine of Reform has never [had] such scope as at the present hour"; the value of "Christianity, the laws, commerce, schools, the farm, the laboratory" was questioned, he said, and not a "town, statute, rite, calling, man, or woman, but is threatened by the new spirit."[3] Certainly, what Emerson observed was only another efflorescence of the American spirit of protest; for as Edmund Burke had pointed out, the very men who settled America represented "the dissidence of dissent and the Protestantism of the Protestant religion."[4] Not surprisingly, then, muckraking was to appear again, after its disappearance in 1912. Even while Parrington and Chamberlain were writing in criticism of muckraking, another wave of muckraking literature was gathering.

History has moved more rapidly since 1906 than Slosson could anticipate; and the critic who writes more than fifty years after his prophecies must perceive not only the blossoming of muckraking in 1900 to 1910, but also its renewed flowering in the thirties and again in the sixties. However, he must also recognize that the literature of exposure is governed by one set of principles and assumptions in the Progressive and Depression periods, but quite another in the sixties.

Muckraking in the Progressive period was the result of four important ideological currents flowing together between 1865 and 1900. This was a period, first, of an enormous increase in Americans' receptivity to ideas. They went to school not only to European thinkers—Darwin, Spencer, Marx, Schmoller, Sir Henry Maine—but also to their own: Lester Ward, William James, John Dewey, Lewis Henry Morgan, and Thorstein Veblen. "The flood of light," as Parrington wrote, ". . . lay brilliant in the intellectual landscape and [even] the dullest mind caught some of the reflection."[5] Eighteenth-century Enlightenment thought had assumed a mechanistic and nineteenth-century Transcendentalism an intuitional series of absolute propositions. Lecturing on "Democracy" as late as 1884, James Russell Lowell had seen only inertia in American social thought. "Things in possession have a very firm grip," he remarked.[6] But by 1900, American thinkers challenged absolutism in the law, society, economics, and the nature of man and his universe, and announced that man was plastic, his moral values experiments, his universe manipulatable, his society dynamic, his economic principles founded on change, and his laws the result of social advance. When existence meant change, faith in reason or intuition—faith itself—was superfluous; only evolution, experiment, chance, and change seemed acceptable. By awakening the mind, this all-but-total shift in ideas provided a crucial context for reassessments of American democratic society.[7]

This logic of possibility nourished the utopian thinking of the late 1880s and 1890s. Beginning with Bellamy's *Looking Backward* in 1888—a book which influenced nearly every one of the muckrakers—utopian projections flourished until the end of the Progressive period, culminating in 1913 in Jeff Hayes's *Paradise on Earth*. As one of the leading muckrakers, David Graham Phillips, summarized the source of this impulse for his age, the "Messiah-longing," he said, "has been the dream of the whole human race, toiling away in obscurity, exploited, fooled, despised."[8]

Social experimentalism and utopian visions joined with the postindustrial recognition of the sad effects of unrestrained capitalism upon the obscure toilers. A foreign observer like James Bryce may have initiated exposure of municipal corruption in the 80s; but he was soon joined by a host of Americans—the Populists, Henry George, William Jennings Bryan, William Godwin Moody, and Henry and Brooks Adams—who showed that the alliance of corrupt politics, predatory business practices, and *laissez faire* had altered American life. Though American politics and business had originated in resistance to anti-egalitarian governments or enterprise, now some kind of regulation was necessary in these, they argued.

These three currents combined explosively in social criticism through the coincidental development of a naturalistic style in literature—one promoted by Howells, practiced by John DeForest, Henry Blake Fuller, Stephen Crane, Frank Norris, and Theodore Dreiser, and designed to depict social relations, rapid change, the flux of experience or ideas, and the character of institutions, all in precise detail. Though long resisted in fiction, naturalism found a popular outlet in the mass media—particularly in the newspapers of E.W. Scripps, Joseph Pulitzer, and William Randolph Hearst, and such magazines as *McClure's* and *Collier's*. All, as Pulitzer wrote of his papers in the 90s, provided vehicles in which war could be waged against the "idle rich" and the "government of the trusts." [9] The new historicism which came from Germany and the naturalistic biography emerging in Germany and England combined with the naturalistic style and point of view to form the muckraking style. No one better stated the principles of muckraking than Lincoln Steffens in describing how he prepared his articles. It was necessary, he observed, "first to clear your mind of all prepossessions, then go to the enemies and the friends of your subject. Take all that they give you of charges, denials and boastings; see the man himself; listen sympathetically to his own story; and, to reduce to consistency the jumble of contradictions thus obtained, follow his career from birth through all its scenes, past all the eye witnesses and documents to the probable truth." [10]

These four developments, occurring between 1865 and 1900, sowed the seeds which the muckrakers harvested in the first decade, their imaginations lighted by the belief that if change was possible, so was reform; and, if reform, then also evolution toward utopia. Emerson had declared that "the history of reform is always identical, it is the comparison of the idea with the fact." [11] Exposing the facts, muckrakers sought to remove the impediments to the ideal.

One need not catalog the muckrakers of this period, and attempts to categorize their activities have always proved futile—for businessmen and poets alike became journalists; journalists, novelists; novelists, historians; and historians, socialist educators. But they had in common a passion for dispassionate investigation, an assumption that the defects of democracy could be remedied by an increase in democracy,[12] and a faith that exposure would manifest truth through public awakening and legislation. "The muckraker's apotheosis," Alfred Kazin has written, "was always the same—a vision of small, quiet lives humbly and usefully led; a transcription of Jeffersonian small-village ideals for a generation bound to megalopolis, yet persistently nostalgic for the old-fashioned peace and the old-fashioned ideal." [13] Above all, they had a simple faith in the worthiness of man, and criticized industrial or political corruption for their corruption of man. They were concerned with institutions—and with perfecting them—because they saw man as pliable, the product of his institutions. Untroubled either by naturalism's emphasis on man's basic animality or by the economic determinism which they professed to believe, and despite the contrary evidence which their own investigations brought forth, they believed, finally, in the excellence of the individual and they wrote to bridge the abyss between the ideas they held and the facts they discovered.

In April of 1906, President Roosevelt named them "muckrakers" and faced them with his prescriptions for expose aesthetics. Two qualities were necessary, he argued—first, honesty ("the attack is of use only if it is absolutely truthful"), and, second, sanity ("No honesty will make a public man useful if that man is timid or foolish, if he is a hot-headed zealot or an impracticable visionary"). Roosevelt's conclusion epitomized the assumptions shared by his targets: "the foundation stone of natural life, is, and ever must be, the high individual character of the average citizen."[14] Their agreement with him was never in doubt. Had not McClure written in 1900 that Josiah Flynt's exposure series, *True Stories from the Underworld*, was "intended to point a moral as well as to adorn a tale"? Would he not, four years later, claim proudly that his magazine had promoted a "high degree of truthfulness, accuracy, and interest"? And did not Mark Sullivan severely criticize *The Jungle* in *Our Times* for being "overdrawn"?[15]

Muckrakers who became novelists appealed to the American habit of tolerance for fiction that aids social progress, and they attempted to write novels reflecting their devotion to utopian ideology, to principles of reform, and to individual worthiness through a commitment to the dispassionate search for truth, honesty in documentation, and sanity. The tradition of the American novel from Poe through Melville and Twain had concentrated on man in extremity. But the muckrakers attempted to create a novel based on the Rooseveltian aesthetics of argument. Creating and treating characters whose biographies needed only to be invented instead of gathered, they minimized the inside narrative of the effect of corruption on either character or action for the sake of the documentation of corruption. As David Graham Phillips remarked, shortly before he died, "Symptoms of the artistic temperament should be fought to the death."[16] Some of the muckraking novelists, indeed, as Van Wyck Brooks said of Upton Sinclair, were so bent on doing good "that they often came to think of artistic truth itself as an enemy of progress."[17] Since they saw man as the product of his external environment, institutions, systems, and organizations became the foci, the true heroes and villains, of their novels, and characters were employed to illuminate the nature of such enterprises in action. Hitherto an imitation of action or character, the novel became an imitation of organizational complexity.

This is not to assert that muckraking novelists simply fictionalized journalistic exposures. No chronological correlation whatsoever could be made between the appearance of a muckraking article and the subsequent appearance of novels revealing the same evil through fiction. Rather, the aesthetic assumptions, the submergence of the aesthetics of fiction into the aesthetics of argument, were primary, part of the imagination of the time, and might emerge into either fiction or journalism. American novelists had portrayed frenzied financiers before 1900—Twain in *The Gilded Age*, Josiah Gilbert Holland, drawing upon the career of Jim Fisk, in *Sevenoaks*, Howells in *A Hazard of New Fortunes*. This is to say, simply, that there was a well-established tradition in American literature of the presentation of the businessman. But the muckraking novelists did not follow in this tradition. David Graham Phillips's portrait of Matthew Blacklock in *The Deluge* of 1905, for instance, followed the point of view of Lawson's *Frenzied Finance* (1904), Russell's *Lawless Wealth* (1908), and Gustavus Myers's *History of the Great American Fortunes* (1910) rather than that of earlier novelists. National political corruption had been excoriated earlier in John DeForest's *Honest John Vane*, Henry Adams's *Democracy*, and F. Marion Crawford's *An American Politician*; but Winston Churchill's *Mr. Crewe's Career* (1907) more closely resembled the aesthetics of Phillips's *The Treason of the Senate* of 1906 or the later exposures of William Hard and Mark Sullivan.

During the 1920s, Norman Thomas quipped, "The old reformer has become the Tired Radical and his sons and daughters drink at the fountain of *The American Mercury*";[18] skepticism, wit, indifference to social issues —these now seemed appropriate attitudes. What had the Progressive period brought, after all, but war? Weren't local and national political leaders as wicked as ever, businessmen as rapacious, and dishonesty as prevalent as in the 1890s? Laughter and mockery were the only weapons.

But during the 1930s, the depression in America and the apparent success of the revolution in Russia produced not only a sense of national disaster but also a sense of the possibility for utopian renewal, which encouraged youth, as Stuart Chase put it "to believe in something again." And again the imagination of the time was lighted by auroras of ideological discovery and stimulated by its vision of the connection between ideas and institutions, theories and actuality. In truth, American intellectual history had developed very little since 1900—but the ideas of Marx, Dewey, Veblen, and Lincoln Steffens still remained potent; Charles Beard, Louis Brandeis, and others whose minds had been awakened in the first decade brought the nineteenth-century protest tradition in line with twentieth-century actualities; European radicalism once more flowed into native channels; and a group of protesters ranging from Big Bill Haywood to Eugene Debs stood forth as examples of Americans' hope for practical reform.

It was inevitable that in this context the writers of the thirties should have looked back over a decade and a half to the muckrakers, to define the writing appropriate to their renewed imaginations. C.C. Regier's 1932 book, *The Era of the Muckrakers*, is a sharp expression of this tendency. After writing the first scholarly survey of muckraking, Regier ended his book by turning from the past to the present, from scholarship to prophecy, from making asseritons to posing a series of questions:

> Is muckraking likely to return? A few years ago the historian would have answered that the era of the muckrakers was a unique phenomena [*sic*] in American history and that the chapter was definitely closed. Today he is not so sure. Liberalism seems to be coming back. . . .
>
> Is there need for further muckraking? . . . Are there any public problems that puzzle the people today? Certainly. . . . At present we find ourselves in a world wide depression. . . . People are beginning to ask fundamental questions. Has capitalism failed? . . . Should our government definitely and finally give up the old theory of laissez faire and actually plan and enforce a unified and harmonious scheme of economic, cultural, and political life for all its citizens? We want to know; and before we can know much we must have the facts; and how can we get the facts except by further honest and scientific exposures? It would almost seem that before we can have another intelligent progressive movement we will have to have some more muckraking.[19]

Regier's prophecy of the renewal of muckraking was as accurate as Slosson's earlier prophecy of its disappearance. Journalists like Edmund Wilson (*The American Jitters*) and James Rorty (*Where Life Is Better*), travelers like Nathan Asch (*The Road: In Search of America*), historians like Matthew Josephson (*The Robber Barons*) and Walter Millis (*The Road to War*), economists like Lewis Corey (*The Decline of American Capitalism*), investigating committees, Nye's and Pecora's among others, film-makers like Pare Lorentz (*The Plow That Broke the Plains*), editors like Heywood Broun, compilers of personal confessions (*The People Talk* or Tom Kromer's *Waiting for Nothing*), analysts of political corruption, of food adulteration, of racial conflict, of prison, and of labor problems—these all paralleled and updated the exposures of the first decade. Both periods shared a passion for truth—in some writers this meant revolutionary awareness created through an understanding of class conflict—based on the material of facts, always more facts, and a commitment to scientific inquiry and sanity in presentation.

The effect on fiction of the return to muckraking aesthetics was immediately apparent. Novels again became what David Madden calls "vehicles for protest and engines for change."[20] Though the return to the muckraking aesthetic in imaginative literature might be signalized in any number of proletarian novels, the four novels written about the Gastonia strike, parts of Dos Passos's *U.S.A.* trilogy, or John Wexley's play *They Shall Not Die*, based on the trial of the Scottsboro boys, the paradigm of the literature produced on these aesthetic principles was, of course, the dramas of *The Living Newspaper*. In Hallie Flanagan's revealing account of its founding, she told Elmer Rice, "We could do Living Newspapers. We could dramatize the news with living actors. . . ." Rice leaped at the idea: "I can get the Newspaper Guild to back it," he said. The staff of the living newspaper, as she describes it, "was set up like a large city daily, with editor-in-chief, managing editor, city editor, reporters and copy-readers, and they began, as Brooks Atkinson later remarked, 'to shake the living daylights out of a thousand books, reports, newspapers and magazine articles,' in order to evolve an authoritative dramatic treatment, at once historic and contemporary, of current problems." Hallie Flanagan called the form "as American as . . . the *March of Time* and the *Congressional Record*"—"as muckraking," she might have said; for its intention, to "dramatize the news," is precisely what Phillips and the earlier muckrakers had accomplished; again, the "big news of the moment" was the exposure of what the living newspaper's editor, Arthur Arent, called "the conditions back of conditions," and Living Newspaper plays were printed with documentation from articles, speeches, and government bulletins.[21]

The Russian Revolution, the war, unemployment, a derangement of social and economic life—these gave writers in the thirties an experience contiguous to that of the working class and a point of view which allowed them, once again, to have their eyes opened to the kind of defects in

American life exposed by the muckrakers in the first decade. And, in consequence, it moved them to adopt the aesthetics for literature promulgated by the earlier age of Roosevelt.

Gathering an anthology of muckraking writing between 1902 and 1912, Arthur and Lila Weinberg asked in 1961:

> Is muckraking being done today?
>   Yes, in isolated instances. Now and then a magazine, a newspaper, a television documentary falls into the best tradition of muckraking. But the concentrated drive for exposure—which marked the opening years of this century—is lacking.
>   Is there a need for muckraking today? . . .
>   We leave these questions open to debate.[22]

Today, the question is not whether muckraking is being done, but whether anything *except* muckraking is being done. An important part of our heritage of the 1930s has consisted in the rising level of sociological sophistication and the consequent penetration of the muckraking aesthetic into every kind of contemporary writing. It is not too much to say that in the late sixties muckraking became equivalent to popular culture.

Let us remind ourselves of the presence and variety of the literature of exposure. Merely to rehearse its varieties is to catalog contemporary culture. Therefore, it is necessary to be schematic and symbolic in naming the kinds of muckraking being conducted today.

Mass Culture is driven by exposure, and on all levels, extending from Vance Packard's numerous works to films like *Easy Rider*, photographic essays like the exposure of the My Lai massacre or those by David Douglas Duncan, magazine articles on all subjects, popular music like Pete Seeger's "Green Is the Grass," and popular fiction like *Airport*. As a theater chain owner succinctly put it, "Once we had this James Bond thing, *Thunderball* . . . and it did this fantastic box office. . . . And now *Putney Swope* is way ahead of it. . . . You can't give them crap anymore. They want social commentary, they want satire, they want a different kind of crap." In the same (Nov. 28, 1969) issue of *Life* which records this observation are: a cover story, "What Ails the U.S. Mails?" an editorial titled "Southern Strategy and Southern Stigma," a profile of "Dr. Jean Mayer, the Nation's Food Watcher" ("Energetic foe of fads and fat"), and a report on the Vietnam Moratorium (one photograph showing a sign reading: "Abolish

Stockades!—Free the Fort Dix 38!—Free the Panther Political Prisoners!"); the issue concludes with "Parting Shots" exposing archaic or repressive laws in America (for instance, "In Atlanta, Ga., it is against the law to loaf. Stopping to tie one's shoe can be considered loafing. $500 or one year").

Though at the opposite extreme in its appeals to an elite audience, avant-garde or "underground" culture has been marked by rapid shifts in interest. The little magazine or quarterly has abrogated the aesthetic formalism of *Poetry* and the cynicism of *The American Mercury* and revived the aesthetics of the Marxist *Blast* and *Anvil*, accommodating politics and economics. Even an antiquarian magazine like *American Quarterly* now proposes to offer articles of "passion and commitment."

Between these two extremes, writing of many kinds incorporates the principles of exposure laid down by Roosevelt—in student newspapers, with their exposures of the administration, the "system," state legislators, the implicit racism of dining-hall menus, and male chauvinism in employment practices; in scholarly muckrakers like C. Wright Mills and Baran and Sweezy, in philosophical muckrakers like Marcuse; in scholarly and polemical muckrakers of education, like Paul Goodman, Edgar Z. Friedenberg, and Jules Henry. Numerous publications devoted to ethnic muckraking range all the way from *The Black Scholar* to *The Liberator*. Legal muckraking, as Judges Hanesworth and Carswell have found, can also attract national attention, and shame some legislators while advancing others. Industrial muckraking has been developed into an industry by Ralph Nader, and "Nader's Raiders" promise to scuttle our "industrial pirates."

But in the late 1960s, some significant changes in the assumptions underlying exposure occurred, which sharply distinguish this from the earlier two periods. Muckraking in the first and fourth decades of the century was ruled by the utopian tradition—a belief in the worthiness of individual man, the assumption that the ills of democracy could be cured by further democratization or by extensions of democracy through Socialism and Communism, and a faith that exposure of ills would bring reform of personal and social behavior.

But the frenzy of exposure and its domination of all aspects of culture has revived the very different, chiliastic tradition of American culture. In 1850, not long after Emerson summarized the reformist tradition, its opposite was defined by his friend, Henry James, Sr., in an essay titled "Democracy and Its Issues": "Democracy . . . is revolutionary, not formative. It is born of denial. It comes into existence in the way of denying established institutions. Its office is rather to destroy the old world, then fully to reveal the new."[23] America, he suggests, was created in and is continued by catastrophe. The contrast between these two traditions occurred vividly in the literature of the late 1880s. The year following publication of *Looking Backward*, Ignatius Donnelly in *Caesar's Column* dramatized the dystopic suspicion that man had already taken irremediable steps toward his annihilation, degeneration, insane confusion. Stumping for Bryan in 1896, he told midwesterners that "the free man will exterminate any new [business] aristocracy which may rise up . . . just as he blotted out the fierce creatures of pre-historic times."[24] Donnelly was not alone in preaching postmillennialism. Clarence King propounded catastrophism in geology; Henry Adams, apocalypse as a theory of history; and Eugene Debs, transformation in political behavior. The tradition continued into the 1930s, when American Marxists stressed class conflict, and followed William Z. Foster's *Toward Soviet America* (1932) in describing the coming struggle for power between plutocracy and proletariat as "cataclysmic." Though the historian may observe the presence of catastrophism in the 1880s and 1930s, this tradition hardly formed a major part of the American imagination. But today, though remnants of the utopian tradition remain as public avowals, our convictions are with catastrophe.

This shift to chiliastic assumptions occurred first and most strikingly in the novel. Somewhat ahead of the most recent resurgence of journalistic exposure, novelists returned in the late 1950s and early 1960s to the tradition of extremity, the dramatization of final possibilities, and they absorbed into their work powerful elements of the apocalyptic tradition. They were not nihilists; they were, indeed specifically concerned with society and social problems, as the earlier muckrakers were. But they could see immolation as the only possible or satisfactory alteration of society. Popular novels and the films made from them—*Fail-Safe, Seven Days in May, Red Alert, Dr. Strangelove*—are paralleled by more serious works of fiction, which are no less dominated by the imagination of extremity.

Certainly, the impulse toward extremity has been present all the while, even in muckraking novels, however hidden by the aesthetic of argument. Do Heller, Vonnegut, Mailer, and others portray mysterious forces, cosmic powers, incomprehensible organizational systems? Here is Frank Norris in *The Octopus* of 1901:

> Was no one, then, to blame for the horror at the irrigating ditch? Forces, conditions, laws of supply and demand—were these then the enemies, after all? Not enemies; there was no malevolence in Nature. Colossal indifference only, a vast trend toward appointed goals. Nature was, then, a gigantic engine, a vast Cyclopean power, huge, terrible, a leviathan with a heart of steel, knowing no compunction, no forgiveness, no tolerance; crushing out the human atom standing in its way with nirvanic calm, the agony of destruction sending never a jar, never the faintest tremor through all that prodigious mechanism of wheels and cogs.[25]

Or, do West, Ellison, Baldwin, Kesey, and Pyncheon describe modern horrors, grotesque urban terror? So could David Graham Phillips:

> She opened a door she had never happened to enter before—a dingy door. . . . At the keyboard [of a piano] sat an old hunchback, broken-jawed, dressed in slimy rags, his one eye instantly fixed upon her with a lecherous expression that made her shiver as it compelled her to imagine the embrace he was evidently imaging. His filthy fingers were pounding out a waltz. About the floor were tottering in the measure of the waltz a score of dreadful old women. They were in calico. . . . From their bleached, seamed old faces gleamed the longings or the torments of all the passions they could no longer either inspire or satisfy. They were one time prostitutes, one time young, perhaps pretty women, now descending to death—still prostitutes in heart and mind but compelled to live as scrubwomen, cleaners of all manner of loathsome messes in dives after the drunkards had passed on. . . . They were drinking biting poisons from tin cups—for those hands quivering with palsy could not be trusted with glass—dancing with drunken, disease-swollen or twisted legs—venting from ghastly toothless mouths strange cries of merriment. . . .
> Susan stood rooted to the threshold of that frightful scene—that vision of the future toward which she was hurrying. A few years—a very few years—and . . . here she would be, abandoning her body to abominations beyond belief at the hands of degenerate oriental sailors to get a few pennies for the privileges of this dance hall. And she would laugh, as did these, would enjoy as did these, would revel in the filth her senses had been trained to find sweet. "No! No!" she protested. "I'd kill myself first!" And then she cowered again, as the thought came that she probably would not, any more than these had killed themselves. The descent would be gradual. . . . Yes—she would come here some day.[26]

Phillips's imagination of catastrophe was suppressed by the aesthetics of argument; he and his fellow muckraking novelists produced scores of novels in which honesty, documentation, and sanity drove out imagination and extremity. Today the aesthetic situation seems to be moving toward the reverse: the novelistic tradition and its impulses of catastrophe, fear, the descent into the maelstrom, govern the literature of argument. Only CBS is willing to bet on "The Twenty-First Century"—and perhaps only because we must have it now—or, we fear, never. When a 1965 issue of *Daedalus* announces that the American utopian tradition has been exhausted; when Paul Goodman calls education "brain washing, on scientific principles, directly toward a fascism-of-the-center, 1984";[27] when radical and ethnic literature assumes power-conflicts, concentration camps, and genocide; when women's liberationists envision utopia as consisting of the extinction of men; when Norman O. Brown and others celebrate liberation through destruction; when ecologists calmly estimate the mathematics of total pollution—then, who can doubt that muckraking has joined with popular culture only to bring the apocalyptic tradition to an apotheosis in our time?

A persuasive example of the way that change is seen as achievable only through the suppression of reform so that catastrophe may occur is in *Movement and Revolution*, a book published in 1970 by Richard John Neuhaus and Peter L. Berger. Neuhaus writes for men who "wonder about the limitations of politics in building the New Order," and gives a "not incredible" chiliastic—and chilling—scenario for a Revolution which could begin "from the corner of Fulton and Nostrand in the Bedford-Styvesant section of Brooklyn." The first phase of revolution, he says, consists of propaganda, disruption, and subversion, including "strategic acts of terrorism"; the second, of guerrilla warfare, including "a campaign to kill, kidnap, or otherwise intimidate any persons or institutions that give the appearance of being effectively concerned about the society's problems. . . . Every appearance of reformism must be discredited"; reformers should be "ceremoniously executed, sometimes with multilation, and frequently with their families." His detailing of the second phase in American terms is highly interesting:

> armed revolution requires the elimination of liberal, counterrevolution-
> ary elements. . . . [Those] who were once useful have become inimical
> to the revolution, not so much in their overt hostility as in their ability
> to persuade people that there is an alternative to armed revolution. The
> more radicalized liberals will welcome first-phase violence as a useful

prod for implementing their programs of reform. But when the revolution determines the beginning of the second phase, the revolution must take the initiative in terminating these alliances, making clear that the issue is joined and the only question is whether one is for or against the revolution. The "best" of the reformers must be ranked with the regime itself as enemies of the revolution. Second-phase armed revolution in the United States at present requires the effective elimination of persons such as Galbraith, McGovern, McCarthy, Randolph, Harrington, Goodwin, Chavez, and, if someone had not already seen to it, Martin Luther King.[28]

Once, institutions and poorly made or ill-regulated laws appeared to be the impediments to the realization of the ideal state, and muckrakers set about removing these. Today, when liberty seems to be a snare and evil a permanent part of human existence, the impediment seems to be man himself, and utopia realizable only through his extinction. We yearn for the end of history, not the renewal, but the removal of man. The literature of argument based on these chiliastic assumptions, it is clear, threatens to abrogate Roosevelt's aesthetic and to give itself to the frenzied, the ugly, the violent, the insane—the aesthetic of apocalypse.

There is no doubt that Roosevelt's aesthetics stripped muckraking novels of their power to move the imagination; equally, the aesthetics of apocalypse would rob the literature of argument of its ability to persuade the reason. Roosevelt was right, after all, in contending that "if the whole picture is painted black there remains no hue whereby to single out the rascals for distinction from their fellows."[29] But he was wrong in demanding that a single aesthetics govern all varieties of the literature of exposure. Like Roosevelt, Americans have always defined their aesthetics monolithically and demanded that an identical principle be applied to every form of literature. By Roosevelt, by McClure, by Phillips, by writers today, the same mistake has been committed over and over again, of confusing the aesthetics of one with the other, and so, confounding both.

These are the dangers of confusing the two aesthetics. The first and fourth decades of the twentieth century brought forth wooden novels; the late sixties inculcate the assumption in much of the literature of argument that only immolation brings renewal and that only our promised end is worth revealing. We ask only whether we will survive to 1984.

Perhaps at all times the imagination needs both the progressive, reformist ability to foresee alteration, and the chiliastic ability to envision transformation. By confusing and collapsing the two we narrow the imagination: without these contraries, there is no advance. Our muckraking literature has not served us as well as it might.

How will it serve us in the seventies? Asking such a question, I give up analysis and, like Slosson, take this opportunity as an occasion for prophecy. Our rising level of sociological, analytical sophistication suggests that exposure based on the principles of sanity and honesty will prevail over the apocalyptic impulse in the literature of argument and strengthen the reformist progressive exposing of the defects of American life. Serious novelists, similarly, seem to have decisively rejected Rooseveltian aesthetics and reclaimed their tradition; the increasing number of readers interested in serious work, increasing literary sophistication, will allow novelists to explore, as deeply and darkly as possible, conditions of extremity.

This is as it should, and must, be—not because sociology is conducted for sociology's sake, and on fixed principles, or art for art's sake, but because both exist for culture's sake; and, by being true to their separate aesthetics, preserve, continue, and advance, as a whole, the culture of which they are separate parts.

In the end I return to Slosson. Muckraking literature, he wrote, more hopefully than accurately, "has taken the tale of facts from the year books and the official reports, from the statutes and decisions . . . and has wrought them into narratives that stir the blood." Such books are art, he said, "because they have power to move him who reads or beholds them."[30]

I share his hope. We need the muckraking analysts and the novelists—even from the first, those of the Progressive period, those of the thirties, those of the sixties. After the conditions they wrote of have been alleviated, even after the writers themselves have perished, our modern world, the seventies, is what they were all the while making for and meaning. If they once moved our minds or hearts, they can do so again, and so move us into our future.

Notes

1. Edwin E. Slosson "The Literature of Exposure," *The Independent*, 60 (1906), 690.

2. Woodrow Wilson, quoted in C.C. Regier, *The Era of the Muckrakers* (Chapel Hill, N.C., 1932), p. 202.

3. Ralph Waldo Emerson, *Works* (Boston, 1883–87), I, pp. 218, 220.

4. Edmund Burke, "On Conciliation with the Colonies" (1775), *Speeches and*

Letters on American Affairs (London, n.d.), p. 93.

5. Vernon Louis Parrington, *The Beginnings of Critical Realism in America 1860–1920* (1930; New York, 1958), p. 402.

6. James Russell Lowell, *Works* (Boston, 1892), VI, p. 36.

7. See Jay Martin, *Harvests of Change: American Literature 1865–1914* (Englewood Cliffs, N.J., 1967), pp. 202–7.

8. David Graham Phillips, quoted in Kenneth Lynn, *The Dream of Success* (Boston, 1955), p. 139.

9. Joseph Pulitzer, quoted in Louis Filler, *Crusaders for American Liberalism* (1939; Yellow Springs, Ohio, 1961), p. 29.

10. Lincoln Steffens, quoted in Harry Stein, "Lincoln Steffens: Interviewer," *Journalism Quart.*, 46 (1969), 733.

11. Emerson, "Man the Reformer," *Works*, I, p. 237.

12. Cf. V.L. Parrington's remark that the "ferment of twenty years ago" created a school "bent on carrying through the unfulfilled program of democracy." *Beginnings of Critical Realism*, p. 403.

13. Alfred Kazin, *On Native Grounds: An Interpretation of Modern American Prose Literature* (New York, 1942), p. 109.

14. Theodore Roosevelt, "The Man with the Muck-Rake," *American Problems*, in *Works*, XVI, ed. Herman Hagedorn (New York, 1926), pp. 416, 422, 424.

15. S.S. McClure and Mark Sullivan, quoted in Filler, *Crusaders*, pp. 73–74, 86, 163.

16. David Graham Phillips, quoted in John Curtis Underwood, *Literature and Insurgency: Ten Studies in Racial Evolution* (New York, 1914), p. 187.

17. Van Wyck Brooks, quoted by Kazin, *On Native Grounds*, p. 110.

18. Norman Thomas, quoted in David K. Adams, *America in the Twentieth Century* (Cambridge, Mass., 1967), p. 273.

19. Regier, *The Era of the Muckrakers*, pp. 215–16.

20. David Madden, "Introduction," *Proletarian Writers of the Thirties* (Carbondale and Edwardsville, Ill., 1968), p. xix.

21. Hallie Flanagan, "Introduction," *Federal Theatre Plays* (New York, 1938), pp. vii, viii, xi.

22. Arthur Weinberg and Lila Weinberg, "Introduction," *The Muckrakers* (New York, 1961), p. xxiii.

23. Henry James, Sr., "Democracy and Its Issues," *Lectures and Miscellanies* (New York, 1852), p. 2. See also James's comment: "Protestantism and Democracy are not so much expansions of the old symbolic institutions of Church and State, as actual disorganizations of them. They mark the old age of those institutions, their decline into the vale of years, preparatory to their final exit from the historic scene." (*Christianity The Logic of Creation* [London, 1857], p. 209.)

24. Ignatius Donnelly, *The Bryan Campaign for the People's Money* (Chicago, 1896), p. 15.

25. Frank Norris, *The Octopus* (1901; New York, 1957), p. 401.

26. David Graham Phillips, *Susan Lenox, Her Rise and Fall* (New York and London), II, pp. 255–56.

27. Paul Goodman, *Compulsory Mis-Education* (New York, 1964), p. 13.

28. Richard John Neuhaus, "The Thorough Revolutionary," in *Movement and Revolution*, edited by Peter L. Berger and Richard John Neuhaus (Garden City, N.Y., 1970), pp. 216–17, 220–21.

29. Roosevelt, "The Man with the Muck-Rake," p. 418.

30. Slosson, "Literature of Exposure," p. 691.

It has been customary for historians to define the era of muckraking as having begun about 1902 (possibly a year or two earlier) and ended about 1912 (certainly no later than the beginning of World War I in 1914). This may be accurate enough in terms of the particular group of magazines, and the men and women who wrote for them, most clearly identified with the kind of journalism that has come to be known as muckraking.

Yet muckraking was a manifestation—somewhat intensified, no doubt —of a kind of journalism, intended to stimulate change and reform, that was observable long before 1902, and that has continued to be evident since 1912. The tradition of reform journalism in the United States has never been totally eclipsed.

Carey McWilliams, distinguished editor of *The Nation*, here traces this tradition from the writings of Charles Francis Adams, John Jay Chapman, and Henry Demarest Lloyd to the present. There is little to add to his discussion, and only minor points in his interpretation with which it would be possible to quarrel. Some would contend that reform journalism goes back to an even earlier point in American history than the period at which he begins to trace it. William Lloyd Garrison and his Abolitionist colleagues might certainly be included. So, perhaps, might Thomas Paine and many editors of the Patriot Press. Some would emphasize other figures and other movements than he has chosen in the contemporary period (1920–1970). But his choices are surely representative.

No living American is so well qualified to discuss this continuing tradition of reform journalism. During most of the last fifty years, Carey McWilliams has been at the center of it. His contributions as a writer and an editor are too numerous even for an attempt at detailing them here. More important, perhaps, have been his never-flagging zeal, his ability to discern those areas most seriously in need of exploration and exposure, his willingness to provide a forum for young and unknown writers.

The Nation, with which he has been so closely identified for so many years, is one of the few periodicals which has consistently served the cause of reform journalism in the half-century that is his principal concern here. The integrity of its editors—Oswald Garrison Villard, Freda Kirchwey, and, most recently, Carey McWilliams himself—has been unquestioned. Its espousal of many different reforms, often when they were unpopular and when *The Nation* stood almost alone in urging them, has provided a first step toward accomplishing many significant changes.

All this is reflected in Carey McWilliams's examination of the continuing tradition of reform journalism.

The Continuing Tradition of Reform Journalism

Carey McWilliams

The existence of a continuing—but cyclical—tradition of reform journalism may be taken for granted; on-going, it seems to disappear at certain times only to surface at a later period.

The reform tradition did not begin with the muckrakers, but the muckraking episode provides a good point of departure. Muckraking journalism had a swift success, a short life, and an abrupt decline. It flourished from, say, 1902 to 1912.

There is general agreement on the major factors which gave rise to muckraking journalism: technological changes which made it possible to reach out for a new mass audience by reducing unit costs; the emergence of a large audience of high-school-educated Americans who were interested in public affairs but found it difficult to relate to such magazines as *Harper's*, *The Atlantic*, *Scribner's* and *The Century*—edited, by their own admission, for "the cultivated classes." More important, a mood of deep social concern and disaffection had emerged. The key to this mood and the political movement it brought into being was a feeling that "the system" itself might be somehow at fault. As Walter Lippmann pointed out, "the mere fact that muckraking was what the people wanted to hear is in many ways the most important revelation of the whole campaign. There is no other way of explaining the quick approval which the muckrakers won."[1] There is also general agreement on the factors which brought about the decline of muckraking. For one thing, the movement of which it was a part tended to merge with the Progressive Party, but, more important, the entire progressive movement, muckrakers and all, was eclipsed by World War I.

The turn-of-the-century muckrakers, however, had their precursors. The articles by Charles Francis Adams on the Tweed Ring and "Chapters of Erie," which appeared in the *North American Review*, helped set the stage. We do not think of John Jay Chapman as a muckraker but *The Political Nursery*, which he edited in New York between March 1897 and January 1901, was as shrewd and realistic about the sources of corruption as anything Lincoln Steffens ever wrote. As Harvey Swados points out, much of what the muckrakers had to say was to be found in Henry Demarest Lloyd's *Wealth Against Commonwealth*, published in 1894.

And there were other precursors. Newspapers had conducted some aggressive muckraking campaigns before the turn of the century. In 1896 Congress was set to consider the Funding Bill, an outrageous giveaway designed to add to the Southern Pacific's plunder. Hearst decided to fight it and, to this end, asked Ambrose Bierce, who was then writing a locally famous column for the San Francisco *Examiner*, if he would go to Washington and direct the campaign against the bill. Bierce accepted with alacrity, and for nearly a year directed an unremitting attack on the Southern Pacific and C.P. Huntington. In his first article from Washington, Bierce wrote: "Mr. Huntington is not altogether bad. Though severe, he is merciful. He tempers invective with falsehood. He says ugly things of the enemy, but he has the tenderness to be careful that they are mostly lies." This was just for openers; Bierce got better as he went along and he kept going for nearly a year. Years later, Charles Edward Russell, one of the leading muckrakers, had high praise for Bierce's caustic assault on the Funding Bill and marked it as an early manifestation of the muckraking impulse. Defeat of the bill marked the first real setback for the Southern Pacific and was a factor in Fremont Older's successful campaign to elect James D. Phelan mayor of San Francisco. Incidentally, when Older launched his campaign against the Southern Pacific in 1896, he discovered that his paper, the *Bulletin*, had for years been the recipient of a monthly stipend from the railroad of which he had not known. Most important newspapers in California at the time received similar stipends.

But while newspapers did participate in reform journalism both before and after the turn of the century, they apparently did not provide the muckraking anthologists with much material. In one sense, as Swados notes, sensational or so-called yellow journalism was a parallel development but much more superficial and not so sharply focused on social issues. Then, too, the newspaper has been with us a basically local institution, largely dependent on local advertising and restricted to a local readership. The issues that began to concern the public at the turn of the century were largely national in character, and we had no truly national newspapers. The muckraking magazines were a distinct journalistic innovation. Taking advantage of the new technology, they cut costs, dropped prices, and reached out for the big new readership that McClure and the others knew existed. The gamble paid off; they got the readership, which in turn produced the advertising. At the turn of the century a new nationwide mass market for certain products was just emerging. But by 1912 the pattern was clear. Once the new mass magazines had demonstrated the existence of the market, other publications moved in and, in effect, took over the invention of the pioneer muckraking journalists. The initial reform impulse, essential to the acquisition of a mass readership, abated once the feasibility of a low-priced mass-circulation magazine, based on national advertising, had been demonstrated. Swados notes, for example, that in a period when radio and television did not exist and we had no truly national newspapers, the new mass-circulation magazines constituted our first mass media. James Playsted Wood, quoting Colonel Harvey, says that the new mass magazines were, in effect, really national newspapers. As he sees it, these magazines wrested from daily newspapers, for the time being, the influencing of public opinion by discussion of public affairs, at least on national issues.[2]

Harvey Swados points out that our country recuperates from the greedy decades "almost like a repentant drunkard recovering from a debauch by trying to examine the causes of his drinking bout and by making earnest resolutions to sin no more."[3] The difference between the nation and the drunkard, he suggests, may lie in the fact that in its moods of sober self-criticism the nation really does redress many of the wrongs, really does help those who cannot help themselves, and does thereby renew its world image as a state concerned not solely, or even primarily, with self-aggrandizement, but much more importantly with dignity, freedom, and decent self-respect. Swados could get quite an argument on this proposition from some of today's rebels and dissenters; nevertheless I share his feeling. *Time*, on September 19, 1969, took much the same position. "For reasons that seem to be rooted in the public mood," it wrote, "muckraking is a cyclic form of journalism. If a society is troubled, it suspects that something is wrong with its system or its leadership; a free press responds by finding out what that is." Conversely, in periods of apparent prosperity and well-being, reform journalism loses its appeal and the muckraking journalist is regarded as a spoilsport or an old-fashioned curmudgeon. But the situation changes when the public—often a new public—becomes concerned over the course of events. These resurgent periods have usually coincided with some change in the pattern of the media which makes it possible for the new concern to find expression. In brief, the reform tradition never dies—there are always a few publications around to keep it alive—but it does seem to fade away at times.

The 1920s were such a period. As the great boom got under way, and the usual postwar frenzies and excitements became rampant, reform journalism receded. Either the reform journals had ceased to publish or their reforming zeal had abated, and the *Saturday Evening Post* and *Collier's*, after the days of Norman Hapgood, were engaged in celebrating the national virtues and pieties. As Wood points out, the reform tradition was sustained during this decade by a group of small-circulation magazines, in some respects more radical than the muckraking monthlies—*The Nation*, *The New Republic*, and one or two other publications. This was a familiar role for *The Nation*; again and again it has helped sustain the reform tradition when the cycle has turned against it. It should be emphasized—because it has been so rarely observed—that Oswald Garrison Villard not only kept the reform tradition alive in the 1920s but also was the major link between the defunct Progressive movement and the New Deal.

For some fourteen years after he went to Washington in 1923, Paul Y. Anderson represented *The Nation* as well as the St. Louis *Post-Dispatch*. In 1924 his first articles began to appear on the plunder of natural resources by the oil industry, and it was not long before these investigations exploded into the Teapot Dome scandal. In 1926 Anderson attacked the oil-depletion allowance in articles referring to oil as "the sacred ointment." The following year he explained how the jury was selected that acquitted Fall and Doheny, and in 1929, of course, he won a Pulitzer Prize for his investigation of what happened to the mysterious $250,000 in Liberty Bonds. He turned in some remarkable reporting on the Chicago Memorial Day Massacre during the steel strike of 1937, and the last days of his life saw him working on articles attacking the Dies Committee. If *The Nation* had done nothing more than publish Paul Y. Anderson in these years it would have made a significant contribution to the continuance of the muckraking tradition. At his funeral, Sen. George Norris said of him, and the words are inscribed on his tombstone: "The pen he wielded for so many years in behalf of humanity, in behalf of justice, was more mighty than the sword of the most illustrious warrior who ever fought upon the field of battle."

Wood also notes, and correctly, that another publication played an important role in keeping the reform tradition alive in the 1920s. We do not ordinarily think of Mencken or *The American Mercury* as part of the tradition but they were, at least during the 1920s. During these years the *Mercury* was like a breath of fresh air. It was lively, irreverent, sharply critical of the dominant dogmas. But it was more of a debunking than a muckraking journal. As the muckrakers had done before him, Mencken discovered a new audience, with new tastes, new interests, new attitudes. Like *The Nation* and *The New Republic*, the *Mercury* was not entirely dependent on advertising revenue. Like these magazines also, the *Mercury* cultivated a new group of writers and encouraged, out across the country, a healthy skepticism. In some respects *The New Masses,* founded in 1926, also helped sustain the reform tradition in the 1920s.

After 1929 the scene changed. The first reactions to the stock-market crash were of shock, disbelief, and bewilderment. Then, rather slowly, a new current of concern and anger began to form. As the decade advanced, the world crisis began to mesh with the domestic, and pressures for change mounted. Old dogmas were questioned and a thirst for new theories and a willingness to experiment emerged. The New Deal was, of course, a response to this mood. On the New Deal and the momentous happenings of the 1930s, the press was divided; that is, the owners and publishers were in general opposed to the New Deal and not inclined to rise to the challenge of the times, whereas the working press was sympathetic and did respond. The election of 1936 is often cited, by J. David Stern and others, as a massive repudiation of the American press. It was not that so much as it was a repudiation of the editorial bias of the press. In December 1932 Drew Pearson's column appeared, and throughout the decade the columnists—Raymond Clapper, Tom Stokes, and the others—offset to some extent the failure of nerve which had beset the publishers, if not the working press.

But it was not publishers alone who experienced a failure of nerve. In his *Autobiography*, published in 1931, Lincoln Steffens not only said that the muckraking tradition was dead but went on to say that it had been a mistake. It had, he thought, stretched out the age of honest bunk and protracted the age of folly. He accused himself of having shared its illusions and of not having realized that muckraking was merely "a reflex of an old moral culture."[4]

But Steffens spoke too soon. In the early 1930s, as he was saying farewell to the muckraking tradition, Matthew Josephson wrote a series of articles for *The New Yorker* about bulls and bears in the market. It then occurred to Josephson to examine their prototypes. *The Robber Barons*, directly in the muckraking tradition, was published in 1934 and has been selling steadily ever since. It was followed by *The Politicos* in 1938, and *The President Makers* in 1940, which extended the same analysis. Books, in fact, seem to have been the prime means by which the muckraking tradition was kept alive in the 1930s, as writers sought to muckrake American history or to give in-depth reports on the state of American life, as Edmund Wilson did in *The American Jitters: A Year of the Depression*, in 1932. *The Grapes of Wrath* and *Factories in the Field* made the nation vividly aware of the social consequences of large-scale industrialized farming and brought the antilabor activities of the Associated Farmers to public attention—without much help from the press. In *The Nation*, Paul W. Ward, Carleton Beals, Heywood Broun, McAlister Coleman, Lewis Gannett, Louis Adamic, and others kept the muckraking tradition very much alive. Radio also played a key role in the 1930s in developing mass awareness of what was happening in the nation and the world. Documentary films were important, as were photographs. The pamphlet, a neglected journalistic form, experienced a rebirth. Dale Kramer's pamphlet on the American Farm Bureau is a fine example of how effective the pamphlet can be. Labor was on the march throughout most of the decade and the great organizing campaigns brought a flood of pamphlet material to public attention. Strikes and strikers were insistent themes. By all these means the plight of sharecroppers, miners, factory workers, the unemployed, small farmers, migratory workers, abandoned mill towns, and tractored-out farm communities were brought sharply to public attention.

Toward the end of the 1930s, an effort was made to found a new-style magazine which was supposed to do for the 1930s what the new mass magazines had done at the turn of the century. *KEN*, as George Seldes explained to *Nation* readers (April 30, 1938), was to be a magazine which would capture a big new labor-liberal-anti-Fascist audience. It was to have a department of the press, headed by Seldes, which would apply a kind of lie-detector to the press. *KEN* was, in a sense, the first attempt to apply a formula with which we have become more familiar with the appearance of *Esquire, Playboy, Ramparts,* and *Evergreen Review*. It remains to be seen how viable and effective this formula proves to be; often the illustrations and the art work tend to get in the way of the content, as Justice

Douglas has no doubt learned. A bitter man, Seldes laid the failure of *KEN* at the door of big business and advertising which, he wrote, "will either change a magazine's policy from liberal to reactionary or try to ruin the magazine." But there is, of course, a third possibility: that readers will buy the magazine for its graphics and its advertising, and ignore its contents.

At the end of World War II we were, as William Barrett has written, "at the end of a long tunnel, there was light showing ahead, and beyond that all sorts of horizons opened."[5] But this bright vision was never realized; instead the cold war intervened. Instead of muckraking, red-baiting journalism became the order of the day. Full of high promise, *PM* was launched, struggled valiantly, and was succeeded by the *Star*, which continued the struggle for a time and then collapsed. *PM* and the *Star* were casualties of the time; to put it another way, they were launched too soon. Throughout the decade George Seldes carried on the old muckraking tradition brilliantly and courageously with his newsletter *In Fact*, which was started because of his feeling that the press had not responded to the needs and challenges of the 1930s. But Wood, writing in 1956, smugly reports the demise of the muckraking tradition:

> Magazine liberalism and iconoclasm have both declined in the years since World War II. The reasons in both instances are apparent. Most of the old idols have been smashed, and the clay feet of newer ones have not yet been identified. Approval of communism, possible and often applauded among the intellectuals in the 1930s and even during the war years, is now dangerous and forbidden. Domestic liberal reform need not be pushed so fiercely. Most of the immediate social gains have been gained, and newer causes either have not been invented or have not been formulated distinctly enough for journalistic clamor. The economically overprivileged class has been abolished through confiscatory income taxes, and a new one has taken its place; the have-nots of the 1920s and the 1930s are the have-its of the 1950s and the immediate future, and the newer tyrants are not yet assailable. The cynicism fashionable a generation ago has been scourged out of the temple in the upsurge of religious emotion reflected in swollen church attendance and in the worship of such newer prophets as Dr. Norman Vincent Peale and Billy Graham.[6]

So it seemed to Wood and to most Americans, perhaps, in the middle 1950s. We were confident we had it made. By then we had become so infatuated with the great god GNP that we could not see the poor and underprivileged in our midst. It took some independent investigators, such as Michael Harrington, Dwight Macdonald, and Herman Miller, to discover them. Even after the Montgomery bus boycott touched off the civil-rights rebellion, the press still failed to zero in on the urban ghettos or to sense what was happening in them. For a decade or more it had, with notable exceptions, been "fighting communism" with an intensity that largely precluded concentration on domestic realities.

It was in these depressing years that the small-media magazines once again kept the muckraking tradition alive. From the middle 1930s on, *The Nation* became increasingly concerned with the mounting world crisis, in part because Freda Kirchwey was always more interested in foreign than in domestic affairs. Perhaps for this reason *The Nation* never joined the great "anti-Communist" crusade and took a consistently critical view of the cold war. Not only did the magazine devote much space to a critical analysis of cold-war policies but it also became increasingly concerned with domestic assaults on civil liberties which were the counterpart of these policies. We devoted major articles to "The Ted Lamb Case," "The Oppenheimer Case," "The Remington Tragedy," "The Hiss Case," and many similar situations. It was rather rough going. When we published a special issue on civil liberties—"How Free Is Free?" (June 28, 1952)— it was attacked by Richard Rovere in the *New Leader* on the ground that by describing what was happening to civil liberties at that time we were in effect giving aid and comfort to the men in the Kremlin.

At the same time *The Nation* pioneered in the application of what might be called muckraking techniques to large-scale arms spending, first in Matthew Josephson's series, "The Big Guns," in 1956 and later with Fred J. Cook's "Juggernaut: The Warfare State" (October 28, 1961). We followed this up with a special issue on "The CIA" (June 24, 1962), the first hard look at that institution. Previously we had devoted a special issue to another *verboten* subject, "The FBI" (October 18, 1958). Prior to the appearance of these issues, the subjects with which they dealt had been generally regarded as off limits. Aside from Max Lowenthal's fine book on The Federal Bureau of Investigation—which came out in 1950, and was in effect suppressed by FBI pressure—the press had failed to take an objective, critical view of the FBI. It had also failed to take a critical view of large arms spending or the CIA. After our special issues appeared, the ice was broken and since then many pieces have appeared on these subjects. Most of these exposes followed in the footsteps of Fred Cook, taking up the same aspects of the subject, in much the same order, and often with remarkably little credit to his trail-blazing efforts.

The Nation did not confine its muckraking to the Pentagon, the FBI, and the CIA. The acute need for old-style muckraking was demonstrated in the special issue—again by Fred Cook—on "The Shame of New York" (Oct. 31, 1956); the title reflects its parentage. This issue led directly to a very fine series of articles in the New York *Herald Tribune*. The last copies of "The Shame of New York" in stock were turned over some years later to John V. Lindsay, who found them useful in a mayoralty campaign he was then managing. We ran one of the first good pieces on cigarette smoking and lung cancer, by Dr. Alton Ochsner, in 1953. We insisted on giving attention to the wicked suggestion that perhaps a tax might be placed on advertising (January 18, 1957, and May 13, 1961). We took a clear hard look at Dr. Frank Buchman (by Richard Harris, May 20, 1961), and at the Rev. Billy Graham (by W.G. McLoughlin, May 11, 1957). When, in 1959, we ran a critical piece on the draft by John Esty, then Dean of Students at Amherst, the Senate Armed Services Committee was so astonished that they invited Dean Esty to come down to Washington and testify. We focused attention on "The Great Giveaways" of the Eisenhower administration in a special issue of that title (October 2, 1954; this article won a Benjamin Franklin magazine citation from the University of Illinois as a meritorious contribution in the field of public service). We ran the first pieces by Ralph Nader to appear in an American magazine, including his article "The Safe Car You Can't Buy" (April 11, 1959). We ran the first of several pieces on the wretched prison-farm system in Arkansas (by Robert Pearman, December 26, 1966). As a matter of policy we tried to throw a light now and then on such sacred American institutions as AT & T—in pieces by Norman Parks, Desmond Smith, Dallas Smythe, Willis Rokes, and Joseph Goulden—and from time to time we suggested that life insurance might bear more scrutiny than it receives from the American press (in articles by James Gollin and Scott Reynolds). We were the first magazine to explore the interesting subject of Jay Lovestone's diplomacy (by Sidney Lens, July 5, 1965) and one of the few magazines or newspapers to feel disturbed about "The Hoffa Trial" (a special issue by Fred Cook, March 27, 1964).

The Nation is not a news magazine. It is a journal of critical opinion. As a publication we are not well adapted to the needs of muckraking journalism. We have a small staff and meager resources. We have no full-time staff writers to assign to various subjects. We are unable to finance extensive research or investigation. To be frank, it was presumptuous of us to undertake such an issue as "Juggernaut: The Warfare State," or the other Fred Cook special issues. Not a penny of foundation money was used to finance any of these projects, although it would have been most welcome. What we did was to build up files of materials, all kinds of materials, and then turn them over to the enormously gifted, hard-working Fred Cook, who is the living embodiment of the muckraking tradition in American journalism. We improvised, we made-do. But we got the issues out, they sold remarkably well, and all of them became in turn best-selling books. We did something else that I think is important and that other small-circulation magazines also do. We brought along many young writers: Dan Wakefield, Gene Marine, Stanley Meisler, Jennifer Cross, J.L. Pimsleur, Robert Sherrill, and many others.

Today, of course, journalism faces a new situation. The scene began to change in 1960, slowly at first, but then it began to accelerate. No journal has a monopoly on dissent today. The change has come about as a result of the two components which have, in the past, ushered in new chapters in the cyclical history of reform journalism: new technology and new interests and concerns. The myth of affluence was beginning to dissipate by the time President Kennedy took office. Nor was it long before a war had been declared against poverty. The acceleration of the war in Vietnam, more than any single event, discredited so-called establishment opinion. The rebellion of blacks and students shattered the complacency which had prevailed. These new concerns created an enormous new market for a modern version of reform journalism. In September 1969 *The Nation* ran a piece by its Washington correspondent, Robert Sherrill, on "The Pendleton Brig," which illustrates the point. That piece was widely reported by the press and by the wire services and was twice used by Mike Wallace on CBS. It brought a House subcommittee to Pendleton almost before you could say "brig." If this piece had been published in September 1967 it would not have attracted the same attention. We have published tougher pieces by Sherrill that received less notice. Once again, as Lippmann pointed out years ago, it is active public concern about a subject that compels the press to pay attention to it. Today new concerns, new apprehensions, new interests have ushered in a new chapter in reform journalism.

The new technology has pivoted on the emergence of television as a major news source. From rather modest beginnings, television news has become a huge enterprise. We are told that for more and more Americans, network news is today their main reliance. At the same time, television began to get more and more advertising that had formerly gone to newspapers and magazines, particularly the large-circulation picture magazines. The reaction was twofold. Newspaper owners began to buy into television when and where they could and, to the extent that they succeeded, took a somewhat more relaxed view of the new competition. But the magazines, notably those hardest hit, began to strike back. In general both newspapers and magazines began to feel that so-called muckraking or investigative journalism presented one of the best means of countering network news.

Insofar as investigative reporting is concerned, the printed media have certain inherent advantages. The printed media constitute a record which can be cited, quoted, filed, and passed from hand to hand, reprinted and distributed in large quantities. Television news is gone in a flash, and it is difficult to get transcripts of network programs. Also it is difficult to present complex situations, with facts and figures, on television. For example, television newsmen, including the producers of some excellent documentaries, concede that the medium has never done a truly effective expose of the military-industrial complex. All news is perhaps a form of entertainment but the entertainment factor is much stronger on television than in the printed media.

But television news has other limitations insofar as investigative reporting is concerned. No one in the industry needs to be reminded that television is a licensed medium, and Vice President Agnew's blast only underscores the point. But that is not all. The fairness doctrine does not present much of a problem to television. But the "personal attack" doctrine, as evolved by the FCC, is another matter. Under this doctrine if a TV documentary refers to someone in a derogatory manner, the producer is under an obligation to seek out this person and offer him a chance, then and there, to respond to the statement. If the person has something to hide, and is sophisticated, he will not accept the offer but will say in effect, "run that sequence and I will sue you." This rule applies, of course, to documentaries, not to news, but it is a cause of much distress to the producers of television documentaries of the kind that might be regarded as muckraking journalism. Then, too, the inability of documentary producers to use concealed mikes or cameras is a serious limitation. Network news is, of course, identified with certain names. These individuals like to project an image of affability, fair-mindedness, and journalistic poise. They do not relish having too many abrasive news items on any one evening's program. Despite these limitations, some fine television documentaries, in the muckraking tradition, have been made: "Biography of a Bookie," "The Business of Heroin," "Hunger in America," "Health in America," "Case History of a Rumor," and NBC's hard look at Mr. Garrison of New Orleans.

But if there is a weakness in television news it is in the area of investigative journalism. Insofar as hard news is concerned, it is becoming increasingly difficult for the printed media to compete. Against this background such papers as the New York *Times* have shown a new interest in investigative reporting. Since February 1967, *Newsday* has had an investigative team, consisting of an editor, Robert Greene, three reporters, and a file clerk, who also functions as secretary and researcher. The team works as a unit. It has its own files and records and separate office. Greene had experience on the staff of the Senate Rackets Committee before he came to *Newsday*. He knows investigative techniques. The team has turned out about three major stories a year, a major story being one that runs for five days, with about 3,500 words for each story. In addition the team has turned out many minor stories. Word of *Newsday*'s enterprise has spread. In 1969 the American Press Institute at Columbia University staged its second seminar on investigative journalism and drew an increase in attendance over the previous year. In February 1967 the Associated Press set up a special assignment team of ten reporters, with an editor. One is a specialist in education, one in health-and-science; the others are all-purpose reporters. In 1969 this team turned out 250 stories; that is, stories that were the product of investigative journalism.

One may hope that the new team of reporters at the AP will remedy, to some extent, a weakness of wire-service news. Again and again the AP has failed to pick up excellent series of articles that have been prepared by local reporters on the basis of intensive investigation. One example is Sanford Watzman's fine series on defense procurement and renegotiation, which appeared in the Cleveland *Plain Dealer*. Another is Nick Kotz's excellent series on meat inspection. There were ten articles in Watzman's original series, but he turned out perhaps fifty stories in the course of the investigation, on which he worked for about a year and a half. There was no reprinting of this series, aside from a "wrap-up" for *The Nation*. The AP did "pick up" four or five of the key stories in the Kotz series, but there were perhaps fifty or more stories in all. Here too *The Nation* and *The New Republic* were able to secure rewrites of some of the material, but it should have had, from the start, much wider national attention. I make it a business nowadays to scan the *Congressional*

Record for series of this kind, which are often inserted by a senator or representative with a special interest in the subject. I learned of the Watzman and the Kotz series in this way.

Nowadays, of course, we have an underground press which is, to some extent, trying to exploit what it regards as the reluctance of the general press to engage in investigative journalism. The New York *Times* of April 3, 1970, reports that the number of such publications has increased from 200 a year ago to 250 or 300 today (see Daniel Ben Horin, "The Alternative Press," *The Nation*, Feb. 19, 1973). In a sense these publications constitute a form of unfair competition since most of them do not pay Guild wages or observe Guild conditions. (Some of them would, incidentally, seem about ripe for organization. There is one in Milwaukee, with a readership of 15,000, which grossed $100,000 last year.) By and large these publications divide into two categories. One group is made up of papers devoted to pot, LSD, and graphics designed to drive mom and dad right up the wall. The other group does show some interest in politics, social protest, and racial incidents. *Nola* and *The Great Speckled Bird* might be cited as examples of this category. In Canada the underground press is beginning to emerge "above ground." There are about twenty such papers in Canada with an estimated readership of 100,000. Photo-offset makes them easy to publish. Copy is set in columns by an electric typewriter, then cut and pasted on a layout sheet. In Canada, 5,000 copies of an eight-page tabloid can be printed for $112.

Then there are many off-beat publications, hard to categorize, which would seem to belong in the muckraking tradition. There was, of course, I.F. Stone's indispensable newsletter. And nowadays the pioneering *Chicago Journalism Review*, which has its counterpart in Montreal's *The Last Post*, has been joined by others (see Don Rose, "Local Journalism Reviews: New Voices of Newsmen," *The Nation*, Jan. 10, 1972). Mention might be made also of Roldo Bartimole's *Point of View*, published in Cleveland, *Inside Media*, the *Bay Guardian*, *Pac-o-Lies*, and newsletters such as the one issued by the North American Conference on Latin America. Then, of course, there is Liberation News Service. What many of these new publications have in common is a savage dislike and distrust of what they regard as "the media," meaning establishment journalism of all kinds, printed and electronic. Muckraking the media has become with them a favorite sport. Then, too, FM radio and documentary films have added something to the muckraking effort; one should mention, also, films such as "Medium Cool," which in a sense was directed at the media.

Several aspects of present-day muckraking journalism require brief comment. Hard pressed for advertising by television, the large-circulation picture magazines have engaged in a form of journalism that in one sense belongs in the muckraking tradition and in another sense does not. It began with a story in the *Saturday Evening Post* about how one football coach had conspired with another. It turned out to be a pretty costly story; a jury returned a verdict of something like $3 million for libel, which was ultimately reduced to $460,000. This kind of story may have helped circulation but, in the end, it did not save the *Post*. But even the best of this brand of journalism has certain troublesome aspects. The original muckrakers tried to expose the system and how it operates. Steffens could be, and often was, on quite good terms with the lawyers, politicians, police chiefs, corporate executives, and legislators whose activities he reported. Robert Greene's team at *Newsday* makes a point of not attacking individuals as such and of letting the facts speak for themselves. Another troublesome aspect is that much of the material for this brand of muckraking, if indeed it really is muckraking, obviously comes from the files of government agencies. This carries an implication that government agencies might be using the media, not to mention the convention that if the information is confidential it should be kept as such and not fed to this publication or that for strategic reasons.

The book remains, today as yesterday, a major resource of reform journalism, but the paperback revolution has added a new dimension to its muckraking effectiveness. In Canada, David and Nadine Nowlan prepared an eighty-page analysis of the Spadina Expressway in Toronto and, thanks to computerized typesetting and offset printing, it was out in three weeks and selling on the stands for $1.25 a copy. The book may force a reconsideration of the project.[7] Many similar examples might be cited to indicate the speed with which books on topical subjects can today be processed, published, and distributed. Frank Graham, Jr., in his book *Since Silent Spring* told of the massive and often personal attacks that were leveled against Rachel Carson when *Silent Spring* was published. Originally *Time* had denounced it as "an emotional and inaccurate outburst" and had accused the author of "putting literary skill second to the task of frightening and arousing readers." But in the fall of 1969, when the government vindicated Rachel Carson by banning DDT, *Time* reported complaints that the ban was inadequate. Graham's book impressively documents the struggle *Silent Spring* had to win a hearing, with a large part of the press attempting to discredit the book and its author.

Ralph Nader's *Unsafe at Any Speed* and Joseph Goulden's remarkable study of the Gulf of Tonkin Resolution are other fine examples of the enduring vitality of the book as a major means of making the truth known against formidable obstacles.

The muckraking or reform tradition is very much alive in American journalism at the moment. But there are difficulties ahead. For one thing, there is not nearly enough of it. Why should it be left to Nader's group of young investigators to ferret out what is wrong with the regulatory agencies? Nader has part of the answer when he says that there are 1,800 full-time journalists in Washington but, for the most part, they are kept so busy reading press releases from federal agencies that they never have time to investigate these agencies. The problem is not with personnel. Today we have some superb investigative reporters: Jack Nelson, Nick Kotz, Sanford Watzman, Robert Sherrill, Bernard Nossiter, Fred Cook, Morton Mintz, Richard Harris, Tom Whiteside, and many more. No, the problem is not with the available personnel—but with how it is used. Good investigative journalism takes time, and money, and commitment on the part of a publisher. If there is a personnel problem it exists at this level. A few more publishers like the late William T. Evjue of the Madison (Wis.) *Capital-Times* would be welcome. Part of the difficulty also relates, of course, to the disappearance of personal journalism. Corporate journalism, of the anonymous newsweekly variety, does not lend itself to good muckraking journalism. Some small newspapers, such as the Tombstone *Epitaph*, publish fine pieces of investigative reporting in their areas with miniscule resources.

Another limitation has to do with libel laws which, although they have been somewhat relaxed, still warn publications, particularly small-circulation publications, away from important subject matter. It has been my experience that individuals and corporations will threaten to sue, and actually sue, small journals of opinion when they would hesitate to threaten or sue the New York *Times* for the same material. On occasion I have arranged for authors to testify before Congressional committees as a means of getting stories before the public, simply because a publication such as *The Nation* cannot afford the luxury of *winning* a libel action. In 1969 we were sued for libel; the case was thrown out of court. But it cost us $7,500 to win it.[8] The quiz show frauds of some years back were very tempting subject matter which we had to forego, not because we were afraid of libel, but because we simply could not afford to defend possible libel suits.

A much more serious problem is: Who will publish the exposes of the future? The magazine industry is caught up in a period of sharp change. *Business Week* (May 2, 1970) reports that the day of the mass magazine, or at least the mass magazine as we have known it, has passed. The "hot" magazines at the moment are those with a special relationship to their readers, that is the selective-audience magazines, whether the audience be surfers, skiiers, or single girls. What this means, as an executive of J. Walter Thompson told *Business Week*, is "simply that print media like everything else that is for sale, are gradually being moved into the traditional and modern marketing mold." Some of the new selective-audience magazines are little more than means by which the publisher, who manufactures products related to the special interest of the magazine, can advertise these products. In such instances the magazine has fused with the advertising and has itself become a form of advertising. Why not call such magazines house organs and let it go at that?

Mass magazines, on the basis of experience to date, cannot compete with television for the so-called "shotgun" audience; the consumer-style selective-audience magazines are all right for advertisers seeking "rifle-shot" precision, but these magazines will not be interested in muckraking except in limited areas. Some magazines hope to make it on subscription income by upping the price to $1 an issue, but this narrows the range if not the size of the audience. As in the past, the small-circulation publications, most of which are in the deficit class, may be required to sustain the muckraking tradition because they are not dependent on advertising and do not need a mass circulation to survive. This creates an opportunity for the newspapers to step into the breach, but will they? And how long will they be able to compete with television for lucrative advertising accounts?

Despite these difficulties, the tradition of muckraking journalism continues and, at the moment, seems to be staging a comeback. Today we have foundations that will occasionally underwrite the kind of research and travel that investigative journalism often requires. The public's appetite for the unbridled truth was never keener. The need was never greater. Also, new technologies seem to be pushing the press in the direction of more and better investigative reporting. And on the horizon are a bewildering variety of technological possibilities of the kind Ralph Lee Smith discusses in *The Nation*'s special issue "The Wired Nation." Muckraking journalism has by no means faded from the scene. It never will—although it may survive in novel forms—because the need for truth never abates.

Leon Trotsky, like Lincoln Steffens, thought that criticism of existing institutions accomplished very little and that, as he wrote in *The Russian Revolution*, its chief function was to serve as "a safety valve for mass dissatisfaction." No doubt it does serve this function. But it is, or should be, a historical constant in any society that aspires to achieve a more rational social order. Steffens and Trotsky to the contrary, reform journalism can be effective. But its effectiveness has come to depend, now more than ever before, on how searching it is and the extent to which it relates the part to the whole, the symptom to the cause. Reasonable cynicism about how much reform journalism accomplishes is a healthy corrective, but total cynicism is stupid and unpardonable. Reform journalists may not be "movers and shakers" but they do edge the world along a bit, they do get an innocent man out of jail occasionally, and now and then they do win a round, sometimes a significant round. A wealth of journalistic experience and much social wisdom is reflected in the title of George Seldes's book, *Never Tire of Protesting*. And we never should.

Notes

1. Walter Lippmann, *Drift and Mastery* (New York, 1914), pp. 4–5.

2. James P. Wood, *Magazines in the United States* (New York, 1956), p. 198.

3. Harvey Swados, ed., *Years of Conscience* (Cleveland, 1962), p. 4.

4. Lincoln Steffens, as quoted in *The New York Times Book Review*, Aug. 31, 1969.

5. William Barrett, "Writers in America," in *The Intellectuals*, ed. George B. de Huszar (Glencoe, Ill., 1960), p. 487.

6. Wood, p. 196.

7. See discussion in *Maclean's* (February, 1970).

8. Three separate actions were filed in the Supreme Court, State of New York, County of New York: Association for the Preservation of Freedom of Choice, Inc., and Donald A. Swan v. Nation Associates, Inc. (index number 8753/1960); Association for the Preservation of Freedom of Choice, Inc., and Donald A. Swan v. George Kirstein, individually, and d.b.a. The Nation Company (index number unavailable); and Association for the Preservation of Freedom of Choice, Inc., Donald A. Swan and Alfred Avins, in his respective capacity v. The Nation Company (index number 1239/1962). All three were eventually thrown out of court, but had to be defended.

Muckraking

Present
and
Future

John M. Harrison and Harry H. Stein

To many observers of journalism in the United States in the latter half of the 1960s, it seemed that a substantial revival of the kind of reporting identified earlier in this century by the generic term "muckraking" was under way. Some suggested that this resurgence would proceed at an accelerated pace and that the 1970s would see the flowering of another "golden age" of muckraking—much like the period from 1902 to 1912.

Exploring this prospect was a principal concern of the conference on "Muckraking: Past, Present, and Future," and almost every participant gave some attention to contemporary manifestations of the muckraking phenomenon. Earlier, muckraking had been the subject for speculation by a number of writers (Louis Filler, Arthur and Lila Weinberg, the late Harvey Swados, and others). Interestingly, when a revised version of Carey McWilliams's contribution to this book appeared in the *Columbia Journalism Review* (Fall, 1970), it was titled "Is Muckraking Coming Back?"

When representatives of the various news media considered the question, "What Is Contemporary Muckraking?" it soon became apparent in these discussions that, although there is general agreement on the proposition that the American society stands in even greater need of change than in the first decade of this century, there is little else on which a consensus could be achieved. It is difficult to arrive at mutually acceptable definitions of terms, or of what is needed to solve present and future problems of the society.

Some disowned the term "muckraking" altogether, preferring "investigative reporting," or just "reporting." Some expressed doubt that exposing injustice and corruption will result in the kinds of change and reform that are needed. There were differing opinions as to whether the established media can or will provide a forum for muckraking. There were conflicting views about the extent to which advertisers are able to influence the decisions of owners and editors with respect to the content of the media.

Commenting on "What Is Contemporary Muckraking?" James Higgins, Professor of Journalism at Boston University and formerly a contributing editor of the now-defunct *York Gazette and Daily* (York, Pa.), raised the most basic kinds of questions:

> There's really no need for investigative reporting today. Corruption is just pouring out all the time. The evidence is already in; the symptoms are overwhelming. . . . There doesn't seem to me to be a social need, a human need, at this particular point for continuing any longer what I would call insignificant fact-raking, or muckraking. The time has come to use our energies . . . toward the employment of facts that are already on the table. They are right there before our eyes.
>
> . . . We have only so much energy. Why waste it in the chase of insignificant facts? I speak as a professional who spent twenty or twenty-one years in the daily practice of reform journalism and the daily practice of chasing the facts which I considered to be pertinent and relevant to human problems. Why not use the energy to reconstruct, to reconvert the society so that the facts we know can be employed to human advantage?

None of the other journalists who joined in the discussion of contemporary muckraking agreed with Higgins, though some did concede that the practice of investigative reporting is often discouraging in terms of tangible results. Dissenting from his suggestion that the information needed to effect reform "is already in," some insisted that such reporting has never been so badly needed. "The nation," declared Arthur Rowse, author of *Slanted News* and a veteran journalist who now publishes the *U. S. Consumer* in Washington, "is desperately in need of muckraking." He went on to support his contention:

> Never before has there been need for so much communication and understanding between people, between races, between the rich and the

poor, between the old and the young, between the effete snobs and the scattershot politicians. We need, more and more, to probe beneath the surface of the news. There is just too little digging for the news in this day and age. I don't think the facts are in yet. We need to know more about what is going on before we come to our conclusions. One of the problems we face today is that people have jumped too fast to conclusions and have decided that our institutions are no good, that what we need is to tear them all down. I go along with Ralph Nader on the point that we have the basis for change within our institutions.

What bothers me is not really the need for more investigative reporting, more muckraking. What bothers me is the great mass of daily developments that are right there for the picking—news that is much needed and wanted by the American people, but simply is not reported to them. . . .

Walter J. Sheridan, an editor for NBC News who has played an important part in several documentaries acclaimed as electronic muckraking, and author of the recently published muckraking study of *The Fall and Rise of Jimmy Hoffa*, took a position slightly different from those of either Higgins or Rowse:

I both agree and disagree with Mr. Higgins. I agree with his frustrations. Too often, you do end up saying "is it worth it all?" But I think I must disagree with some of his conclusions.

Some of the major disclosures that you read in the daily newspapers didn't just surface. They were the result of long and hard hours of work in investigative reporting. Traditionally, in a democratic society, the government and the institutions are supposed to serve as watchdogs of the community, along with us. But too often they don't, because they are uninformed, or because they aren't able to do it, or maybe they are corrupt themselves. And, by the same token, too often the news media don't do it either. . . .

Denny Walsh, who won both Pulitzer and Sigma Delta Chi awards as a reporter for the St. Louis *Globe-Democrat* before joining the investigative reporting team of *Life* magazine and who is now a reporter for the *New York Times*, offered yet another point of view of the importance of muckraking:

As far as people not realizing the depth to which social reform should go and the long overdueness of this social reform, most of them probably do realize these two things at some point in time, but they forget it. They might realize it today because of something that somebody has told them, or something they have read. They might realize what's going on, but tomorrow they have forgotten for the most part. So I would really hate to see the people who are doing the muckraking in this country vacate, turn themselves to the task of rebuilding from the ground up, and leave what I believe would be a vacuum. Because . . . the support which the rebuilding must have from the populace would dry up in a very short time, just because of people's short memories of how it was before. So we need the people, regardless of how few the victories are and how insignificant some of the facts may seem, to keep reminding people what's going on. The facts may be in, but let's keep them there. Let's not walk off and turn our backs on them. . . . They're going to be forgotten. Let's keep them on the table where, Mr. Higgins maintains, they are now.

All who took part in the discussion of present and future muckraking—with the exception of James Higgins—could and did agree that there is greater need than ever before for the kind of journalism that exposes faults and abuses in the American society and its institutions. This need, they agreed, will continue to grow, as the society becomes more and more complex. These faults and abuses need to be explored in even greater depth and with greater perception.

Nathan Blumberg—professor of journalism at the University of Montana, former dean of the School of Journalism there, and author of *One Party Press?*—in his discussion of "Muckraking in the 1970s" ticked off a whole series of targets for future muckrakers:

Now that it is acceptable—indeed, even politically and economically advantageous—to favor ecological decency, the muckrakers of the 70s surely will include far deeper exploration into this cancer. Most of us realize that we have only begun to dig beneath the surface that Rachel Carson and others scratched years ago—an exercise, not incidentally, for which they were either ignored or excoriated by the news media of the time. . . .

We can anticipate, for the first time in the history of the American mass media, serious examination of the structure, policies, and practices of privately owned electric power utilities. . . . The unconscionable pollution practiced by these companies will have to be curbed, and there is no hope . . . that these monsters will voluntarily undertake programs quickly and effectively to curb the poisons they belch into the air in every part of the country. . . . Then, when the muckrakers of the 70s explore this putrescent problem, they are certain to see the relationship of these utilities, which exploit our natural resources for the economic benefit of a very few, to our tax problems. . . . Furthermore, when the long-delayed investigation by the news media is under way, journalists of the 70s additionally will expose the pernicious political influence of these companies on our municipal, state, and federal governments. . . .

The new muckrakers can add studies of the unwonted influence of these corporations and their agents on the university systems of several states. . . . The rake might be drawn through the muck of the corruption of the legal profession, in which large numbers of lawyers become beholden to, or fearful of, the corporations. . . . But now that the eyes have been cast down to the pile of manure resulting from the activities of lawyers, it becomes but a logical step to a reappraisal of our courts, our judges, our entire judicial system. . . .

But we are just getting started. While examining our courts, we unquestionably will see how black men, and brown men, and red men, and poor white men fare in the dispensing of justice. Then stare at our black ghettos—a sight uncovered for large numbers of shocked and disbelieving whites only in the last decade. Move on, then, to those red ghettos—the reservations. . . . The Indians themselves, with no significant help from whites or from the white news media, have set about to correct this situation. If the news media were to do their duty, the major reforms could be achieved in the first half of this decade, and an unparalleled blossoming of the magnificent cultures of those tribes would be a joy to all Americans of conscience and good will. . . .

Muckraking in this decade will delve into our systems of education —public and private, elementary and secondary, undergraduate and graduate. Especially will the relationship between the universities and the federal government be explored, to explain what is now the minority viewpoint, held by some academicians, that the university should be beholden *in no way* to the federal government.

The agenda for muckraking in the 70s will include the practices of the slumlords and the real estate agencies whose record and potential for inflicting misery is one of the many shames of our cities. . . . The time is long past due for the press to investigate the conditions of the powerless in their struggles against the powerful in matters of simple economic justice. What flashes to mind is the California grape strike. Almost two years ago, I termed the coverage of that strike "a continuing national disgrace," and the coverage since that time has made quite clear the fact that the orthodox media support the growers. In this case, a kind of blind madness permeates the media. . . .

Muckraking in the 70s will concentrate heavily on an examination of United States foreign policy. What will occur, it seems safe to predict, is not a call for simply a revision of our current practices, but a wholesale turnabout in the policies and the ways in which they are implemented. For instance, the secret deployment of American nuclear weapons overseas. That would lead directly to an examination of the role of the U. S. government and its agents in the death of democracy in Greece. Ad infinitum.

Although journalists recognize the need to attack on many fronts to achieve reform and change, yet, they have serious doubts and reservations concerning the likelihood that this challenge will be met by the news media. Many see the need for profound change, even revolutionary change, especially in how the news media see their role in effecting reform.

What is important in muckraking, suggested James Higgins, is not to be found by examining it "in terms of approach, of technique, of style, of even that imaginative leap which novelists are supposed to make, but which I have known many reporters to make also," but to look at it in terms of "what is the purpose, what is the intent of any kind of work of words."

As Eldridge Cleaver said: "Either you are part of the solution or you are part of the problem." And Eldridge Cleaver wasn't talking about muckraking journalism, but he was talking of a purpose, he was talking about human beings, and everything in the long run is a personal question because we don't die socially, we die individually, personally. And so I speak the way Eldridge Cleaver puts the question. Either you are a part of the problem or you are a part of the solution. "Part of the problem or part of the solution" has to do with the helpful approach to what muckraking investigative reporting in journalism, or in any other area of words, is all about.

Nathan Blumberg believes muckraking will flourish in the 1970s:

The reason I believe muckraking will become an ultimately crucial factor in the second American revolution is that control of the content of the orthodox media will be wrested from the publishers and taken over by trained journalists who have some sense of fairness, justice, and— finally—news values. What will come . . . is the recognition by working journalists that they are part of the problem when they should be part of the solution. Journalists already are profiting from the lessons learned by the students on our campuses and our streets; by the blacks and the Chicanos and the Indians who have begun to fight their way out of oppression after decades of subservience to an unresponsive system. They cannot help but learn from our Catholic brothers; if the priests have challenged the Curia, then it will not be long before copy editors challenge Copley.

Nick Kotz—formerly a member of the Washington bureau of the Des Moines *Register*, now with the Washington *Post*, a Pulitzer Prize winner, and the author of a widely acclaimed study of hunger in the United States, *Let Them Eat Promises*—took up this theme in commenting on Mr. Blumberg's remarks:

I'd like to start off . . . where Professor Blumberg left off, and I agree with much of what he said. He said what is needed now, and desperately needed, is the recognition by working journalists that they are part of the problem when they should be part of the solution. He suggested in very general terms that somehow reporters are going to get on the side of justice rather than injustice, on the side of decency rather than indecency, and so on, and right on! I think it's a far more complicated proposition than that. I know he knows it is. He was talking about an agenda for action and I'm going to tell you that there will be no agenda for action unless there is some serious rethinking about what journalism is all about and how to do it, because two things are badly lacking in American journalism today.

These two things that are lacking, Kotz asserted, are any willingness by journalists to go to "the heart of power, the heart of institutions, the heart of motives," and the failure to communicate what is found there in terms that relate directly to the needs and wants of the people who comprise their audience. Because they are lacking, Kotz is not optimistic about the prospect that the news media, as they exist in this country today, can or will provide a vehicle for "explaining to people how this country really operates."

All who took part in these discussions agreed that the media are not doing what they might do, and should do, to explain to the people how this country really operates. Arthur Rowse, after citing half a dozen or more examples of developments of interest to most Americans as consumers—all easily available to the media, but largely unreported by them—offered these observations:

Why don't the big, powerful, rich news media—even the noncommercial media—pick these things up for the asking? Why don't they report these to the American people? The real answer is not the cost of doing this job, although the news media say it is. The material is already there. I can report it without any staff. The chief reason is something more basic. It's a matter of antiquated news concepts.

By and large, the news media are operating under the old two-alarm philosophy that has been in effect in this country for at least 50 to 100 years. This results in an overemphasis on violence, scandal, tragedy, amusement, for the sake of drawing people to advertising. . . .

The second major reason for the failures of the news media is the fear of displeasing advertisers. This fear is unjustified by the facts. . . . In most cases where the conflict has developed, the news media have proven more powerful than the advertisers. The advertisers need the media more than the media need the advertisers. . . .

The final reason for this failure to perform better is the problem of technical limitations. These include the need for action film on television and the impossibility of obtaining enough of the right kind, plus the great expense of producing documentaries, which are television's greatest journalistic device.

Walter Sheridan, of NBC News, agreed with Rowse's analysis of the reasons why the news media—specifically television—are not doing more of the kind of reporting that can be described as muckraking. He suggested another factor that too often is missing:

> If an organization is going to do this kind of job, it's got to have not only the willingness, but really an eagerness, to do it, and it's got to have guts, to spend money and take the time to search out and back up competent investigative reporters. It has got to be willing to take the political guff and to withstand the pressure from advertisers. . . . And the reporter himself must be patient, must be a person of integrity, must have contacts and develop sources.
>
> Where are we now? I think, for one thing, we are intimidated. Agnewism has taken its toll. At a time like this, when the First Amendment is under attack, there is a greater need than ever for us to be doing our watchdog job. John F. Kennedy once said that one man can make a difference. I don't think there is any field in which this is any more true than in the field of muckraking, or investigative reporting.

Another explanation of why the news media fail to dig into and expose conditions—especially in their own communities—was offered by Denny Walsh. The pressure to refrain from this kind of muckraking journalism, he contended, is not usually overt. Most of the stories which gave *Life* a reputation for significant contributions to investigative reporting, were available to newspapers in the communities where they originated. He suggested this analysis of the reasons why they had not been reported:

> The owner and/or top officers of the newspaper in almost every case have financial, civic, political, and social entanglements with their selected segment of the community in which the paper is located. And this makes it extremely difficult at times for a muckraker to surface the transgressions of this segment of the community, even though there are things about it that should be exposed. You can barely walk through a city room [of a newspaper] without tripping over some sacred cows. The number of powerful persons dependent on this nation's press for advertising and good will is growing every day, mainly because they are smart enough to take the publisher and top editors and owners of these newspapers into their own little select circle. And then it's not long be-

fore these people begin to think that what's good for the people around them is good for the community. And the people around them are the Establishment. The editors make their homes right in the middle of their circulation area; that's unavoidable. Their wives belong to the same bridge clubs with the wives of the men appearing in the pages of the newspapers; maybe that's unavoidable, too. The children go to the same school; that's unavoidable. And the men go to the same masseur; maybe that's unavoidable. But I say that no publisher, editor, or owner of any newspapers in this country should be an officer, a director, or a major stockholder—or even a minor stockholder—in any local corporation, or even a corporation that just does business in that town and is headquartered elsewhere.

The question naturally arises as to whether it is fair to the journalist —if you can call these people that—to expect him to sacrifice his financial interest. Why should we say that it's the duty of the editor to make enemies, if necessary, in giving the public news and in performing other kinds of community services? Why cannot the editor run his business as other men conduct theirs, in the manner that will insure him the greatest return? The answer, of course, is that the newspaper is not merely a business concern—or it shouldn't be. In the very nature of things, it cannot do the job it is supposed to do if it is run on the controlling principle of business—that the good will of everybody is the basis of success. There are simply too many people in my profession who are unwilling to take the losses—personal losses, not corporate losses, financial or otherwise—that are sure to come from a policy of representing the interests of the unorganized public against those of powerful individuals and groups. They represent the dead weight of somebody with an honest instinct for muckraking.

These strong indictments of the news media by so many journalists, with recurring emphasis on the pressures—both inside and outside— which restrain and limit the investigative function of journalism, would hardly seem to suggest conditions favorable to the burgeoning of a new "golden age" of muckraking. Where, then, is this journalism of exposure and reform to find an outlet? If owners and editors of the media are interested only in profits and thus loath to risk incurring the displeasure of advertisers, if they are a cozy and comfortable part of the Establishment, and if—especially in the case of the licensed electronic media—they are cowed by the implied threats of government spokesmen, it must seem unlikely that they will permit their properties to be used for muckraking journalism. What alternatives are there?

Nathan Blumberg's prediction—that "control of the content of the orthodox media will be wrested from the publishers and taken over by trained journalists who have some sense of fairness, justice, and—finally —news values"—is not so preposterous as some might think. In Europe, there are already notable examples of control by journalists, with the excellent Paris newspaper, *Le Monde*, as the most strikingly successful example. Many editors and publishers throughout the United States have been confronted in recent years by demands from some of their ablest young reporters that a bigger say in day-to-day editorial decisions be granted to working journalists. And though there is no example of their being given full control, in a number of instances these younger journalists have been able to exert a strong influence on both the policies and the content of newspapers (the Boston *Globe* is perhaps the best known example).

Even when there has been no striking and dramatic change, there have been instances in which the upper echelons of management have responded to discontent among members of their working staffs by taking steps to improve the internal situations of their newspapers. More than a few have managed to ease out of key positions those troglodytes whose outdated ideas and concepts have stood in the way of the practice of vigorous journalism, replacing them with younger and more progressive men. It was the thirty-one-year-old executive city editor of the Rochester *Times-Union*, Philip R. Currie, who played a key role in decisions that authorized two young reporters on his staff to dig into the circumstances surrounding the deaths of several guards held hostages in the Attica prison riots, revealing that they had been killed by guardsmen's bullets, not by prisoners—a reportorial effort that won them a Pulitzer Prize.

There are, finally, at least a few employee-owned newspapers (the best-known and most successful is the Milwaukee *Journal*). Usually this has been possible only when a family line of ownership has run out. Even then, more often than not, such properties have been snapped up by eager, profit-minded buyers. While newspapers remain as remunerative as most are today, the likelihood that their employees can bid successfully for ownership is minimal.

It must be conceded that today—nearing the halfway mark in the decade of the 1970s—there is little tangible evidence to support Blumberg's optimistic prediction that a "new breed of journalist" will take over control and operation of the news media. That forces which might bring about such a change are at work is certainly possible. But there may be other, more promising alternatives.

To most of those who discussed prospects for contemporary and future muckraking, the most often-mentioned possibility was the "underground" press. The term itself is imprecise, since few are "underground" in the original sense of publication outside the law, though many have undergone harassment of various kinds. They differ greatly in both content and appearance, defying any attempt to describe them in general terms. What most of them do have in common is a concern about some of the problems that might logically engage the attention of muckraking journalists in the 1970s. Some are devoted almost wholly to a single problem; others have more general concerns.

These "underground" publications also vary in the degree to which they depart from the orthodox press in appearance, style, and content. A few, like the *Village Voice* in New York and the Los Angeles *Free Press*, have built large circulations and grown prosperous. They have become, in the eyes of some, more nearly akin to the established press than to the "underground" publications for which they once served as models. Others continue to operate on a hand-to-mouth basis, with limited numbers of readers, little or no advertising revenue, and frequent suspensions of publication—sometimes temporary, sometimes permanent.

James Higgins is an enthusiastic advocate of this segment of the press as a logical source of present and future muckraking:

> There is a press in this country which seems to me actually and potentially suited to the time. I refer, of course, to the so-called underground press, which is another way of saying that it is the press of, by, and for the youth. And it is a press read not only by the youth, but read by them to the exclusion of much of the conventional press. This is another fact that we ought to have some awareness of. I think that what the youth are trying to say here in the underground press is . . . that there have got to be deep and strong institutional changes. They are making this known, not through the kind of pursuit of fact that we are accustomed to associate with competent journalism but, for the most part, through screams and cries of rage, although you will find fact in the underground press. . . . But we don't find the fact there that we are accustomed to finding in the conventional and established press.
>
> What interests me is how little attention of a really serious nature we pay to the underground press. I wonder how many journalism schools offer courses in the underground press. I wonder how many of the scholars here, instead of investigating the great muckraking period of fifty, sixty, or seventy years ago, have ever considered taking a look at the contemporary underground press as a field of serious study. The quality of the reporting and writing is, by our standards, often poor and weak, with some notable exceptions. There are four or five excellent

investigative underground newspapers. What they do, week in and week out, is to put very heavy emphasis on the facts that are important —the facts about war, the facts about racism, the facts about poverty, etc. They exhume consistently what I would call the stinking cadavers of our institutional and, yes, our personal lives. If the underground newspapers are disgusting—well, what does this say about us and our institutions?

To be aware of contemproray muckraking . . . I would refer you to the underground press. That's where contemporary muckraking is both actually and potentially at.

Arthur Rowse did not specifically discuss the "underground" press, and he would no doubt object to classification of his *U. S. Consumer* as part of it. Yet in the sense that he makes it his responsibility to report developments of interest to the nation's consumers (events that are available to, but largely unreported by, the "orthodox" press) his publication does have much in common with those that purport to do a part of the job that the established news media largely neglect. Rowse's contribution to this discussion of contemporary muckraking was, for the most part, a detailing of the many instances in which *U. S. Consumer* has done exactly that. In at least one observation, he clearly supported the rationale for the "underground" press:

If the media were doing a better job, a more adequate job, of reporting and interpreting the daily flow of events, there would not be a need for so many auxiliary and supplemental news services. These institutions are not really geared to handle the news, yet they are doing it. There might not be such widespread public dissatisfaction with the news media themselves and, indeed, I think that society might not be faced with quite so many of the urgent problems that are thrust upon it, seemingly so suddenly and seemingly without warning.

Walter Sheridan, too, had some kind words to say about the role of the "underground" press, though he saw it as a supplementary, rather than an alternative, vehicle for muckraking journalism:

I do think the young people and the blacks are a new force in muckraking. They have raised some questions that we should have been raising. I agree with Mr. Higgins that the underground press is a necessary and vibrant thing in our society, but I think we are really either talking about evolution or revolution. If we're talking about revolution, then maybe the underground press is the only answer. I still believe in evolution. And if evolution is going to work, the only way it's going to work is through the legislative process, through the correction of faults in our institutions and our government. The only way that's going to happen is by way of public opinion, and the only way that will happen is for the news media to get across to the public. Unfortunately, nobody but the kids read the underground press.

Not so, Denny Walsh responded in his discussion of contemporary muckraking. Commenting on the part played by the "underground" press, he declared:

> They're not just shouting. There can be a strong case made for the fact that one of the major income-tax-evasion cases in recent years was exposed by the underground press in San Diego . . . which printed a story about how the Nixon Administration was trying to quash a long-standing income-tax investigation of one of the more prominent citizens of the Southwest—a man by the name of John Alessio. After three articles (and I say there are more than kids who read the underground press; I know Mr. Nixon saw these three), Alessio and four of his brothers were indicted on a multimillion-dollar tax-evasion charge, which will probably have a very healthy effect on San Diego County in the long run. Well, why didn't the San Diego *Union* use this story? It was available. . . . It's a shame, really, that the underground press had to do this. It cast a long shadow on the daily press in that part of the country.

It was obviously a basic assumption of those who took part in this discussion that newspapers—both "orthodox" and "underground"—should carry a major share of responsibility for present and future muckraking. But what of the magazines—the medium that served as the vehicle for much of earlier muckraking? They were mentioned. Walter Sheridan, for example, commended *Life* as a "very forceful, courageous vehicle in this field," citing specifically its exposures of the links between Senator Edward V. Long of Missouri and James R. Hoffa, and the extralegal activities of Supreme Court Justice Abe Fortas. And Denny Walsh, in talking about his experiences as a member of *Life*'s investigative team, cited reasons why a national magazine may be able to do this kind of reporting more easily than most newspapers can, or do. Discussing the exposure of Senator Long's ties with Teamster President Hoffa, Walsh declared:

> That story was available to the St. Louis *Post-Dispatch*, as it was available to . . . the other two major daily newspapers in Missouri—the Kansas City *Star* and the St. Louis *Globe-Democrat*. I don't want to minimize the effort of *Life* . . . but the abuse of the Senator's power could have been documented by any of the three newspapers in Missouri

who had the money and the power to do it. They all three had their reasons why; in the case of the *Post-Dispatch* they did not want to disgrace what they considered to be Ed Long's good cause—the exposure of snooping on the part of various government agencies. . . .

Sidney Zion, who was involved in trying to get the ill-fated *Scanlan's Monthly* off the ground, had some pertinent things to say about the problems of muckraking magazines. In recent years, he suggested, those that have engaged in muckraking have usually done so in a desperate effort to reverse downward trends in both advertising and subscription revenue:

> What ordinarily happens in a situation like this is that your editorial content changes because you tend to panic—what the late Howard Gossage used to call "flop sweat." Like the old vaudeville comedians who got out on the stage . . . they'd tell a couple of jokes and if they didn't go over they'd start to get mad at the audience for not laughing, and then the whole thing would just blow apart. That's the kind of thing that happened to the *Saturday Evening Post.* . . . It is interesting to have a magazine like the *Saturday Evening Post* to talk about because it's nice to kick that around; it's nice and dead now and nobody cares about it. But they had a magazine that a lot of people liked and read, and then, when the ads started going down, they decided to go in for muckraking, but they didn't tell their readers that or ask them whether they wanted a muckraking magazine, having had Norman Rockwell for all these years. . . . When did America ever have seven million people who cared about muckraking?

Zion made no attempt to answer his own question, and apparently he was unaware that the total circulation of the earlier muckraking magazines had been—in proportion to the population of the United States at the time—well above the seven million he mentioned. His purpose in citing this figure as unattainable was to support the belief of those involved in *Scanlan's* that its goal should be an audience of about 500,000 readers.

He suggested, too, that a muckraking magazine cannot rely on advertising revenue as a major source of support because "if you start worrying about advertising . . . you're going to limit the area in which to muckrake." Illustrating his argument, Zion declared:

> You can go after the Mafia, because they don't advertise, or you don't know whether they're advertising for sure. And I suppose if you're lucky enough you can occasionally catch a judge, because they don't advertise; they aren't allowed to. They probably would if they could,

and if they could, nobody would investigate them. Maybe that's the way they should have changed those legal ethics after the Fortas case. They should have said, "from now on lawyers and judges can advertise and nobody will expose them." Imagine the story conference saying, "How could we do this to Abe Fortas; after all there are those two pages every month that come in here. . . . And what about all the other judges? They'll stop advertising and we'll lose the bar association. . . ." That's the next thing you'd get. . . . And it would be one more story that never happened.

It is tempting to speculate on the degree to which Sidney Zion's observations—especially those concerning the demise of the *Saturday Evening Post*—were prophetic of what has happened since May 1970. There are obvious parallels with the death of *Life* in December 1972, for here was another magazine "that a lot of people liked to read" which had modified its original concept in several ways as advertising revenues had begun to decline, turning eventually—just as had the *Post*—to a kind of journalism that was widely identified as muckraking. So had its principal rival in the area of photojournalism—*Look*, which preceded *Life* in suspending publication. Thus, all three of the last remaining mass-circulation magazines (the *Readers Digest* is generally regarded as a special case) had turned as a last resort to their own versions of muckraking journalism, which had saved none of them. Is the lesson to be drawn that muckraking and a mass audience are incompatible? Perhaps, though the failure of Zion's own limited-circulation periodical adds a complicating factor in making generalizations.

In this discussion of present and future muckraking, television was occasionally mentioned, though not as much as might have been anticipated. No one took up the late Harvey Swados's imaginative proposal that television represents the logical medium for muckraking today because it is most nearly comparable—in terms of access to the public—to the popular magazines of the early twentieth century. Nathan Blumberg did specifically suggest that there is reason to hope it may:

> The 70s will see television networks regularly and consistently committed to muckraking. They will blossom as the tired old men move on—Chet Huntley to Montana, which he *does* understand; Howard K. Smith to an earned retirement, Eric Sevareid to whatever pasture he wishes to graze in. . . . The newsmen of this decade already show signs of being a different breed of cat, and I venture to say that he will be a cat who will not be averse to jumping in the muck.

Other references to television, however, were generally to express reservations concerning its potential as a muckraking medium. Those who did mention the possibility agreed that the format of daily television news programs does not lend itself to the in-depth reporting that is essential. Instances of effective exploration of serious problems cited were documentaries, and few saw much hope for the expansion of these kinds of programs. Walter Sheridan, recalling his own experiences as an investigative reporter for NBC News, suggested one of the limitations:

> The way they did it—and I think it's the only way you can do it—was to break off a group of people who do nothing but that, who do specials, or white papers—whatever you want to call them. In the day-to-day news, television is not really suited to get into a complicated story because they just don't have the time. The only answer is to have more sixty- to ninety-minute specials where they can dig in depth into a subject.

A partial refutation to this argument may have been provided by CBS News during the 1972 presidential election campaign in its treatment of such controversial matters as the Nixon administration's handling of the grain deal with Russia, and the forcible entry and electronic bugging of Democratic national headquarters in the Watergate complex. In each instance, a series of relatively long segments (seven to twelve minutes) was presented as parts of the daily CBS Evening News programs. To some extent, these were largely comprised of recapitulations of material that had already appeared elsewhere, but each focused attention on charges that had been made and, especially in relation to the Russian grain deal, included the results of CBS's own investigative reporting that might certainly be characterized as in the muckraking tradition.

Many newsmen are pessimistic about television's role in muckraking. Even the news departments of the three major networks do not have the personnel to carry on the kind of investigation that is essential. Most network executives regard their news operations as incidental to entertainment and advertising, which are inextricably linked to put top priority on attracting the largest possible audience. As for local stations, only a very few maintain staffs large enough to do special news programs. They simply do not probe into problems—even those of major local importance.

Another alternative medium—although it is not usually grouped with newspapers, magazines, television, and radio as news media—was mentioned frequently. Books, it was contended repeatedly, have become one of the most effective vehicles for muckraking in recent years. Carey Mc-Williams has stressed their importance in his essay "The Continuing Tradition of Reform Journalism." Arthur Rowse, referring to McWilliams's observations, suggested that "all we have to do is to look at the books of the past decade—by Ralph Nader, Rachel Carson, Norman Dacey, and a few others—to see that a lot of the news we get today is not coming from the daily news media, but from books. . . ."

Walter Sheridan specifically cited the importance of Ralph Nader's work, in its various forms, as representing a "whole new dimension," a "one-man campaign [that] has filled a vacuum that the news media should have been filling, but weren't." And Denny Walsh, indicting local newspapers for their failure to report what is going on in their own communities, added this comment:

> I suppose the question has already been posed, but it stands as a classic example now: Why in the world did it take a man like Ralph Nader—a private citizen in the context of our discussion—to expose the dangerous corner-cutting indulged in by the auto industry? Where were the Detroit newspapers all those years? They were sitting right on top of it. It wasn't hard to document.

To students of the muckraking tradition, Ralph Nader has represented a kind of anomaly, ever since his *Unsafe at Any Speed* was published in 1965. In his books, in his testimony before congressional committees, in his lectures to audiences throughout the country—especially in colleges and universities, where he has been a kind of hero—he has raised new issues, loosed new charges, and generally performed the role of muckraker and gadfly. The forays of his teams of "raiders" into problems and institutions of every sort are a legend of our times. A recent contribution —a voluminous study of the operations of the Congress of the United States and its individual members—is strongly reminiscent of that older, and equally controversial, muckraking work, David Graham Phillips's "The Treason of the Senate." Yet, as Walsh pointed out, Nader has worked in the role of private citizen, not as a part of the news media. They have transmitted his messages widely, but usually at second hand— reporting his latest activities extensively. Whether Nader points the way to a new expression of the muckraking impulse, with others emulating his example, or whether he is indeed a unique phenomenon remains undetermined. Few would question that in the 1970s he continues to be the single most effective exponent and practitioner of the muckraking tradition.

The contributions of other books to effective muckraking were favorably mentioned by both Nathan Blumberg and Nick Kotz. Citing the need to examine the "structure, policies, and practices of the privately owned electric-power utilities," Blumbreg observed that "Senator Lee Metcalf and Vic Reinemer, in their splendid (and largely ignored) book, *Overcharge*, have documented in excellent muckraking tradition the ways in which electric utilities mislead and exploit almost all of the citizens of this country." Kotz gave special praise to James Ridgway's *The Closed Corporation*, as an example of effective muckraking of the nation's universities.

Blumberg noted another medium not usually mentioned in discussions of muckraking that offers an outlet for those who would bring about change in the society and its institutions. That was film and, he suggested:

> The young and the young in mind have seized the cinematic art of communication as their own. "Easy Rider" and "Medium Cool" and "Z" are only the beginning; even Hollywood's cheap imitations—"Midnight Cowboy" and "Alice's Restaurant"—contain enough grit to make them candidates for the outer fringes of muckraking in the 1970s. The cinema of relevance is yet another reason that the print media will be forced to abandon outmoded, essentially irrelevant patterns of news coverage.

There was general agreement among all who took part in this discussion on at least one proposition—that not enough muckraking is being done. The reasons why there is too little reporting that probes deeply into the maladies of our time were suggested over and over again in their comments—pressure from advertisers, politicians, and other sectors of the public; the identification of media owners and editors with the very people and institutions that should be exposed; outmoded concepts of what is news; failure to report what is happening in terms that will have meaning to those who make up the media audience. But they had few solutions. As Denny Walsh succinctly put it:

> We've given you a lot of problems, but very few answers. What do you do? Strike? Nationwide? I don't know whether that would work against the barons of entrenched greed or not. . . .

Nathan Blumberg professed to see changes coming in the seventies that would result in a "continuing repudiation of many basic beliefs and traditional values." He went on:

It will be a period of violence and barricades. In the words of Orson Welles, "It's gonna shake the fat cats until there's nothing left for them to sit on." But I suggest it also will be a decade of a flowering of the human spirit. After the liberation of France, Albert Camus emerged with his underground newspaper to the light of a new day. "Out of the dread childbirth," he wrote, "a revolution is being born." I believe, in deepest sincerity, that the press of this nation will stand, in the tradition of the muckrakers and in the words of Camus, "not for power, but for justice; not for politics, but for morality."

Nick Kotz took up this concept, though it did not lead him to so optimistic a conclusion:

> I liked Professor Blumberg's quotation from Camus. It seems to me that the reason Bob Kennedy always got a rise when he ended his speeches during the last six months of his life with another Camus quote was because it communicated something very, very meaningful to people that they could understand about the human condition. That was the quote in which he said: "It may not be possible" (I'm paraphrasing loosely) "to stop the torture of the children in this world, but if we do not make an effort to reduce the torture, to see that there are fewer tortured children, then who will?"
>
> That is the basis of the ethical action that I take as a journalist. I'm not as optimistic as Professor Blumberg is that if the American society were being described—if its institutions were being described as they really operate—then we would have revolution in this country today. I am not so optimistic as to think that if meaningful institutional examination had been going on for twenty years, our problems would be a lot less. But I do think that if organized society in America has any chance of surviving at all, the role of the press will surely be to operate from an ethical base, to operate from fundamental principles of decency which are in the charter of this country. That has got to be a given. But the main role of the press . . . has to be as a vehicle for explaining to people how this country really operates.

A plaintive note recurs persistently in these comments. The need for the kind of reporting that has come to be identified as muckraking was never so great as it is today. Its philosophical underpinnings are so simple, so uncomplicated. Nick Kotz summed them up admirably in those two descriptive phrases—the press must "operate from an ethical base" and it must be "a vehicle for explaining to people how this country really operates." Why, then, should these men—all of them practicing muckrakers in one way or another—be so pessimistic about the future of muckraking?

It is obvious that, on the whole, they have lost faith and confidence in the willingness of the news media to accept and implement these two essential elements. Most of the media do not "operate from an ethical base," and most do not serve as a "vehicle for explaining to people how this country really operates." That is a chilling conclusion at any time; it is especially so at a time when there is such critical need for journalism based on these tenets.

One might hope that Nathan Blumberg had been accurate in predicting basic change—even revolutionary change—in the media during this decade. But one is more likely to share the skepticism of Nick Kotz, Denny Walsh, and others that such change can be effected in a society which seems—except in rare instances—to be more concerned with wallowing in its affluence than with probing the problems that beset it.

This exploration of present and future muckraking points up the imperative need for a new professionalism in the news media, replacing the commercialism that has been their guiding principle. Whether this can be accomplished without the kind of revolutionary change suggested by Nathan Blumberg and James Higgins, no one can say. All the media have formulated professional codes that provide bases for change. Few among them have made any serious attempt to implement or enforce any of the provisions of these codes.

Muckraking reporters win many of the awards that are presented every year to print and electronic journalists. Some schools of journalism imbue their students with the conviction that thorough investigative reporting is the single most important function of the news media that will employ them. Spokesmen for all the media exhort their contemporaries to provide complete information about the society in which we live. A few—a very few—attempt to perform this function.

Looking back on the developments in this decade since these discussions took place, one is at first struck by a sense of disappointment and disillusionment. Some surely would note a significant irony in the fact that three of the five publications represented in the discussions which explored contemporary muckraking have gone out of existence—*Scanlan's Monthly*, interred after only a few issues; the *York Gazette and Daily*, sold, renamed, and transformed within a year; *Life*, closed down in December 1972. Three down in three years—hardly an auspicious omen for the future of muckraking.

An examination of Nathan Blumberg's challenging "agenda for the 1970s" in the light of what has been accomplished is little more encouraging. There has been no great surge, to date, of the deep and searching examination he foresaw in such areas as the privately owned electric-power utilities, the courts and justice systems, the educational systems, the practices of the "slumlords and real estate agencies," economic justice for the underprivileged, "ad infinitum." There have been tentative probes in some of these areas, but nothing to match Blumberg's predictions.

"The times they are a changing," Bob Dylan had sung, and many Americans believed in May 1970 that the forces of change—especially the young people—were about to achieve great successes. The rhetoric that was so pervasive at the time echoed again and again in the statements of participants in these discussions—manning the barricades . . . action in the streets . . . new values . . . new concerns . . . new priorities . . . even a new journalism!

But now, in the wake of a national election in which the very forces that were to lead the way in all these changes have been resoundingly beaten, the atmosphere is a very different one. It is an atmosphere of repression, in which dissent seems never to have been so completely out of official favor. Fewer than six weeks after that election, a Nixon administration spokesman announced that legislation was being drafted which would hold local television stations accountable for maintaining balance in the network programming they offer, implying that licenses might be denied on this basis. This obvious attempt to widen the existing rift between the networks and their affiliated stations could scarcely encourage already jittery television executives to expand the kind of investigative—and almost inevitably controversial—documentary news programs so often cited as the electronic media's major contribution to the muckraking tradition.

New threats, too, have been posed to the print media in the form of a series of court orders and decisions compelling reporters to reveal information, and the sources from which it is obtained, which has provided the basis of news stories. In some instances, it is not easy to defend on principle the use of the kinds of materials which comprised these accounts— sensational and sometimes poorly documented as they have been. But the very possibility of much investigative journalism rests on a confidential relationship between the reporter and his sources. If these court orders, citations for contempt, and jailings that have seemed to be ever more numerous should continue to multiply and eventually to be sustained, many believe that a crippling blow will have been dealt to muckraking, that its sources of information will have been dried up.

Yet, it should also be noted, the tradition of muckraking dies hard and the sheer volume—in all its various forms—probably is greater today than it ever has been. If the 1970s have, thus far, produced no "golden age" of muckraking, there are many individual instances to suggest that the tradition continues to find expression.

Jack Anderson's syndicated "Washington Merry-Go-Round" column is the single most dazzling exhibit—appearing regularly in almost 1,000 newspapers, the number increasing with each new muckraking venture. Since he took over the column in September 1969 from the late Drew Pearson, with whom he had been associated for more than twenty years, Anderson has been cited repeatedly as the outstanding "muckraker" of the times. And he has scored his most devastating hits in the last two years—first with the publication of secret White House documents revealing the Nixon Administration's duplicity during the India-Pakistan war, then with publication of the Dita Beard memo, suggesting that the Justice Department had made a favorable out-of-court settlement with the International Telephone and Telegraph Corporation in an antitrust case, in return for $400,000 toward the cost of the Republican national convention. These revelations won for Anderson a Pulitzer Prize, along with more customers, more readers, and other financial increments.

It is true that many journalists, along with many government officials, regard Jack Anderson as too often unreliable and untrustworthy—a muckraker in the more negative connotations of the term. And he provides his critics with frequent supportive evidence, as when he broadcast last summer the unsubstantiated report that Senator Thomas Eagleton, then the Democratic vice-presidential nominee, had been arrested for drunken and reckless driving in the 1960s. Admitting that he had not seen documents to support the allegation, but had only been told of them, Anderson sought to rationalize his irresponsible action by explaining that he feared he would be "scooped" by some other journalist if he failed to make public the unsubstantiated charge against Eagleton.

Even so, the impact of Anderson's more solidly based muckraking activities since 1970 certainly suggests that the effect of this kind of journalism of exposure has not lessened. If additional evidence to support this conclusion be needed, it has been provided by publication in the *New York Times*, the Washington *Post*, the Boston *Globe*, and several other newspapers of the Pentagon Papers in 1972. Whether the excerpts from these documents, providing a detailed review of U. S. actions in Vietnam over a period of several years, actually represent muckraking in the traditional sense may be debatable. Presumably, muckraking goes beyond publishing classified materials—even when they have been carefully edited and annotated. But if exposure is an important element of muckraking, as most would agree it is, there have been few instances in American journalism in which the spirit of muckraking has been so obviously manifested. The publication of these papers and the litigation that has ensued raise many questions: about the propriety of revealing the contents of documents that may well have been illegally appropriated, about attempts by the government to impose prior censorship for the first time in almost two centuries, and about a suggestion that the Supreme Court—while upholding the right to publish in this particular instance—might sanction the suppression of other materials in other circumstances. But in terms of what actually happened in this instance, publication of the Pentagon Papers does stand as an outstanding example of journalism in the muckraking tradition in the 1970s.

There is, finally, the not yet completed story of the crimes attendant to the successful effort to re-elect Richard M. Nixon as President of the United States, conveniently identified as "Watergate"—the name of the office and residential complex in Washington where the headquarters of the National Democratic Committee were burglarized in the early hours of a June morning by a group of men in the hire of the Committee to Re-elect the President. But for an all-out investigative effort, carried on in the best muckraking tradition, the nation might never have known more than the relatively insignificant facts that burglary and electronic surveillance had taken place.

The role played by two young reporters for the Washington *Post*—Bob Woodward and Carl Bernstein—in digging out the facts behind that incident already has been acclaimed many times over as one of the shining moments in the history of American journalism. Supported and encouraged by the *Post*'s executive editor, Benjamin C. Bradlee, and its publisher, Mrs. Katharine Graham, Woodward and Bernstein kept at the job through months when they were almost alone in seeking to reveal the whole Watergate story; months during which they and their newspaper were under continuing attack by the Nixon administration and its spokesmen. (For a full account see the *Columbia Journalism Review*, July/August 1973, pp. 8–22.)

Although it has sometimes been marred by questionable practices, this painstaking investigation into closely protected events, places, and people —in which the *Post* eventually was joined by many others—is surely deserving of all the awards and accolades that have been accorded it. Seldom in the nation's history has the press performed its investigative function so admirably, against such overpowering odds. Even President Nixon and his spokesmen have conceded that point, however grudgingly.

If muckraking is, indeed, properly identified as the "journalism of exposure," then the Watergate story is ample proof that there is no lack of muckraking enterprise in the United States today. Others along with the Washington *Post* and its two young reporters must share in the credit for slowly bringing out the truth. And, in all probability, considerable parts of the truth may never be told. But the investigative effort that went into revealing what is now known represents another historic landmark in the muckraking tradition—one so exceptional that it offers strong evidence of the continuing health of that tradition.

The electronic media—especially the television networks—have continued to produce occasional muckraking news programs. Few documentaries have stirred greater controversy than CBS News's *The Selling of the Pentagon*, shown twice in 1971—the second time with an appended segment reflecting the nature of the controversy. Although it contained relatively little information that had not already appeared elsewhere, this indictment of the Defense Department's public-relations activities—often in direct contravention of official regulations—fulfilled all the specifications of effective muckraking. It resulted, too, in further threats from political figures—Vice President Spiro Agnew, and Congressmen Harley Staggers and F. Edward Hebert, among others—to impose various kinds of restrictions on the network news operations. And those involved in its production were compelled to spend countless hours documenting and explaining various aspects of its contents and editing procedures, including a demand that CBS turn over to a congressional committee all unused film footage—a demand that was successfully resisted. But if the harassment were intended to discourage the networks from continuing to present such documentaries, it does not appear to have been wholly successful. As recently as December, 1972—only a few days after the announcement that legislation was being drafted to hold the networks' affiliated stations accountable for programming balance—NBC News presented *What Price Health?*, a hard-hitting exposure of the costs and inadequacies of medical care in the United States which gave little comfort to the Administration, the Department of Health, Education, and Welfare, or the American Medical Association.

What, finally, can be said of muckraking in the 1970s? It is obvious that a balance must be struck somewhere between Nathan Blumberg's optimistic predictions at the beginning of the decade and the gloomy forebodings of those who have proclaimed the death of muckraking. No revolutions have been accomplished in our institutions—not even in the news media. At this particular time the political climate seems decidedly unfavorable to investigation and exposure, while the public attitude is, at best, ambivalent and unpredictable. Yet muckraking journalism continues to appear in all the various news media, and efforts to suppress it have generally been thwarted. Newspapers may neglect many opportunities, but publication of the Pentagon Papers and, even more dramatically, the development of the Watergate story are notable muckraking achievements of the 1970s. Ralph Nader and Jack Anderson provide examples of muckrakers who, though they may use different methods, are at least as devastating in their attacks on corruption and privilege as the Steffenses and Phillipses of an earlier period ever were. A healthy number of magazines continue to investigate and expose, despite the demise of some, and the trend toward periodicals with limited audiences and special interests may yet produce successes where *Scanlan's Monthly* failed. Network television does resist attempts to discourage its muckraking proclivities; public television offers tentative support, hobbled as it is by its dependence on government funding; cable television, its direction still uncertain, opens up whole new vistas of muckraking possibilities. Books and movies continue to make their contributions. And the "underground" press, though it has failed to live up to the bright promise many professed to see in it only a few years ago, goes on probing into areas where the orthodox media fail, attracting as staff members some of the brightest and ablest of the younger journalists, who do not seem deterred by low salaries and uncertain futures.

Never a static phenomenon, muckraking today shows signs of both continuity and change. The impulse is the same as that which produced a journalism of conscience in the first decade of this century. It may take new forms; it may address new audiences; it may displease people in high places who may seek to suppress it. The reports of its death, however, have been decidedly exaggerated.

LIST OF CONTRIBUTORS

RORERT C. BANNISTER, JR. Associate Professor of History, Swarthmore College. Author of *Ray Stannard Baker* and various articles.

NATHAN B. BLUMBERG. Professor of Journalism, University of Montana. Author of *One Party Press?* and various articles. His paper, "Muckraking in the 1970s," was presented at the conference and is often quoted by the editors in their closing chapter.

JOHN G. CAWELTI. Professor of English and Humanities, University of Chicago. Author of *Apostles of the Self-Made Man, Six-Gun Hero* and various articles; co-editor of *Sources of the American Republic*.

DAVID M. CHALMERS. Professor of History, University of Florida. Author of *The Social and Political Ideas of the Muckrakers, Hooded Americanism* and various articles; editor of *The Muckrake Years*.

IRIVING DILLIARD. Ferris Professor of Journalism, Princeton University. Former editor of *The St. Louis Post-Dispatch*; author of *The Development of a Free Press in Germany*; editor of *Mr. Justice Brandeis, Great American, The Spirit of Liberty*, and *One Man's Stand for Freedom*.

LOUIS FILLER. Professor of American Civilization, Antioch College. Author of *Crusaders for American Liberalism; Crusade Against Slavery, 1830–1860; Randolph Bourne; Dictionary of American Social Reform* and various other books and articles.

JOHN M. HARRISON. Professor of Journalism and American Studies, The Pennsylvania State University. Author of *The Man Who Made Nasby, David Ross Locke* and various articles; co-author of *Mass Media and the National Experience*; editor of *American Newspapermen: 1790–1933*.

CAREY MCWILLIAMS. Editor of *The Nation*. Author of *Ambrose Bierce, Ill Fares the Land, Factories in the Field, Prejudice* and other books and articles.

JAY MARTIN. Professor, Program in Comparative Culture, University of California, Irvine. Author of *Harvests of Change, Conrad Aiken, Nathanael West* and other books and articles.

HARRY H. STEIN. Visiting Scholar, The Annenberg School of Communications, University of Pennsylvania. Author of various articles.

INDEX OF NAMES